WALT WHITMAN'S DRUM-TAPS

AND

SEQUEL TO DRUM-TAPS

WALT WHITMAN'S
DRUM-TAPS
(1865)

AND

SEQUEL TO DRUM-TAPS
(1865-6)

A FACSIMILE REPRODUCTION

EDITED WITH AN INTRODUCTION

BY

F. DeWOLFE MILLER
University of Tennessee

GAINESVILLE, FLORIDA

SCHOLARS' FACSIMILES & REPRINTS

1959

SCHOLARS' FACSIMILES & REPRINTS

118 N.W. 26TH STREET

GAINESVILLE, FLORIDA

HARRY R. WARFEL, GENERAL EDITOR

REPRODUCED FROM COPIES IN

AND WITH THE PERMISSION OF

HOUGHTON LIBRARY, HARVARD UNIVERSITY

L. C. CATALOG CARD NUMBER: 58-9955

MANUFACTURED IN THE U.S.A.

LETTERPRESS BY WAYSIDE PRESS

PHOTOLITHOGRAPHY BY EDWARDS BROTHERS

BINDING BY UNIVERSAL-DIXIE BINDERY

To

CHARLES E. FEINBERG

INTRODUCTION

THE AUTHOR AND THE BOOK

Early in the Civil War, Walt Whitman gave the name of *Drum-Taps* to a handful of manuscripts of what might be called reveille poems. Later from time to time he added others which can be called wound-dresser poems. All of them were gathered into a volume in 1865, but it was no sooner completed than Lincoln's assassination made it incomplete, and Whitman withheld the volume so that in its *Sequel* he might add a funeral dirge.

He did not know, and indeed no one has ever remarked the fact, that the title conceived at the beginning contained a comprehensive irony that made it appropriate for the sad finality of the national experience—Lincoln's death and the myriad others it stood symbol for. It was not by the bugle but by the drum (and thus the word *taps*) that the military taps were first sounded. The word was already in use by the time of the war, but *tattoo* was the common term; even as late as 1888 Whitman, though he knew the meaning well, was not quite sure that he did. On the death of Sheridan in that year Walt had sent an elegiac poem, "Interpolations," to the New York *Herald.* Numerous other papers copied it, substituting their own title, "Taps." Whitman, who at that moment appeared to be mortally ill himself, asked Traubel, "What are taps? I have a dim notion of the truth in my brain but I am not confident I know. I want you to ask the first soldier you meet. . . . As I guess at it now it is a . . . last sort of ceremony before turning in—the final message of the drums before sleep. It has a certain kind of solemn significance" (WWC, II, 144).

PIVOTAL IMPORTANCE OF DRUM-TAPS

Drum-Taps was not the only thing that was wrenched from its original intention. Whitman himself was affected. The war years had a marked influence in many strong and some subtle ways on both his life and his art. This was the second most important pivotal point of his career, the greatest experience he had had since his conversion in his late twenties from prose to poetry. Nothing in Whitman's life can rival that remarkable conversion; it is in fact virtually unique among major poets, for the others grew into their art from very childhood. But barring this remarkable passage in Whitman's career, the period of the most significant changes is that covered by *Drum-Taps*.

In one sense we can even say that this was the most important volume that Whitman published. It is the greatest book of war lyrics ever written by a single author. It contained in "O Captain! My Captain" one of the ten best known English poems (*Granger's Index*). It contained in "When Lilacs," a poem that has ever since been considered—what the founder of the New York *Times* early called it—one of the loftiest products of human meditation. Last and least, *Drum-Taps* contained in "Chanting the Square Deific" a poem which Whitman and some of his intimates often regarded as his most significant utterance. No mean record, that, for so slight a volume. Yet virtually all readers would prefer that the world had *Leaves of Grass* 1855 than *Drum-Taps*. It is altogether possible, however, that without *Drum-Taps* very few of us would have ever had the perspicacity to find the rest of Whitman out.

WHITMAN IN THE WAR YEARS

Material for the study of Whitman increases dramatically with the beginning of the Civil War. The biographer of the pre-war Whitman has to depend largely on the published writings for a judgment of Whitman the man, in whom, quite apart from his poetry, a personal interest inheres. After the war began, the number and variety of primary materials increases in geometric

leaps. Five times more letters survive from 1863 than from all
his previous life together. Notebooks, diary entries, scraps of
all sorts of manuscripts, the beginnings and early versions of
poems,—all these survive from the whole war period in quantities
far greater than those of earlier years.

It is not the intention here to give a full biographical account
of Whitman during the years he was writing *Drum-Taps*. It will
be possible to study only the facts directly related to the composition and publication of the volume, set in an outline of data
concerning his goings and comings. Though the primary biographical material is far more abundant than for previous periods,
there are nevertheless some problems which have yet no satis-
factory explanation. During the first twenty months of the war,
Whitman very strangely wrote a group of recruiting poems, most
of them apparently in the first burst of enthusiasm, and then—if
we simplify the dates—proceeded to adopt a mode of life and
writing almost deliberately calculated to free his mind of the
conflict.

His notebooks and diaries, the list of articles published
during the time, and other miscellaneous sources indicate that
he spent most of the time that can be accounted for (1) visiting
the Bohemian literary circle in Pfaff's beer cellar, (2) riding up
and down Manhattan on the omnibuses and street cars, and taking
numerous brief notes about the drivers—notes almost entirely
unrelated to the war, (3) making a rare trip or two into the
country districts of Long Island, and (4) writing nostalgic
articles about Long Island, Brooklyn, and Manhattan and its
hospitals, which in subject and tone were for the most part
escapist.

The Questioning of Whitman's Patriotism

Contemporary critics of course held Walt accountable for all
this in one way or another, but no organized questioning of it
came until the 1930's when William E. Barton published *Abraham
Lincoln and Walt Whitman* (1928) and Harvey O'Higgins got

Beat! beat! drums! — Blow! bugles! blow!
Through the windows — through every door — burst like a
force of armed men
2 to the solemn church, and scatter the congregation,
2 to the school where the scholar is studying,
Leave not the bridegroom quit — no happiness now with his bride,
Nor the peaceful farmer any peace, ploughing his field,
fierce you whirr and pound, or gathering his grain,
so strong you drums — so loud you bugles —
bugles blow.

A Nearly Final Draft of the Most Representative Poem
from the Early Group (*Drum-Taps*, p. 38)

Courtesy of Charles E. Feinberg

a hearing in *Harper's Magazine* (May, 1929) for an irresponsible and undocumented attack. Charles E. Glicksberg, in *Walt Whitman and the Civil War* (1933), brought out a miscellany of uncollected materials and unpublished memoranda and letters, making a better knowledge of Whitman's activities possible.

The sympathetic critic who wishes to rationalize Whitman's conduct must work more on faith than on facts. My own faith prompts me to suggest that, more really than is usually supposed, Whitman, after the first flush of patriotism felt by so many at the time, suffered a period of bewilderment which he did not afterwards admit, even perhaps to himself. The opening lines of the earliest known draft of a poem of the period seem rather specific:

> Quicksand years that whirl I know not whither
> 1861-2.
> years that whirl I know not whither
> nothing is sure

Thus it would be from suffering—anything but indifference— that Whitman would seem to be indifferent, suffering because of the dilemmas that such a war could present to such a man. His articles on old churchyards, the family names on tombs from long ago, scenes from Manhattan of the past, the Old Bowery Theatre and Booth in his prime—all of these, as well as Pfaff's beer cellar and the Knickerbocker omnibus, give their suggestion that Walt Whitman was fundamentally disturbed, that he was not a superficial patriot such as could have written the first drum-tap poems, that he was not—as we sometimes assume—a digest of the greatest common denominators in the year's headlines. We have today achieved a perspective from which any such hesitancy in the presence of any side of any war can no longer be reason for disparagement. Whitman was certainly so shaken that he had to reassure himself:

> nothing is sure . . .
> Only the theme I sing, the great Soul,
> One's-self, that must never be shaken—
> GLICKSBERG, 126

As he felt the "quicksand years, slipping from under" his feet, he may have found it quite necessary to escape to surely established periods of history by writing, quite literally, of Brooklyn's snows of yesteryear. Following by only a few years his emphatic celebration of the present as compared to the best the past or future could offer, this new penchant for reminiscence certainly needs explanation, and it may be that some truth lies hidden here. The suggestion is not entirely new, for I find that I have by my own route reached an understanding close to the masterful explanation of Emory Holloway, made before the modern critics of Whitman began to carp (1926, pp. 192-3).

GENTLE HIGGINSON ATTACKS GENTLE WHITMAN

A charge which called into play the title of the book itself was made that Whitman was willing to sound the drum taps but unwilling to respond to them. The charge was not made by an irresponsible man. It was made by the gentle Thomas Wentworth Higginson, never in his long good life given to attack or invective except here. The casual reader today is apt to assume that the matter first came up during the Civil War when the issue was still alive. But no one had apparently ever noticed that Whitman had not volunteered, until Higginson twenty years afterward reviewed the 1881 edition of *Leaves of Grass*. He then elaborated the reasons why a man who bragged of consummate health and called on all others to fight should not have remained at the comparatively remote distance of the hospital.

During the rest of his life, even long after Whitman's death, Higginson continued attacking Whitman on this as well as on some other counts; this pertinacity revealed the only approach to fanaticism in the life of a man whom many admirers of

Whitman admired—and the list includes from the inner circle
the names of Burroughs, Traubel, and Kennedy, all of course with
qualifications.

An obituary, which Higginson apparently prepared ahead
of time and deposited in the morgue of the New York *Post* to
await Whitman's death, contained one of his numerous repetitions
of the charge. Of the many hundreds of obituaries this was the
most widely distributed, the most elaborate, the most damaging.
Three important national journals copied or extracted it, the
Independent editor having added it to his own attack with obvious
glee (*Evening Post,* March 28, 1892; *Nation,* LIV, 262-4;
Independent, XLIV, 479-80; *Current Literature,* X, 81-5). Cir-
cumstances of publication make it obvious that this obituary was
on file awaiting Whitman's death. We quaver at the inhumanity
of the best of men when we conjecture that it was prepared
during Whitman's critical illness three years before.

William Sloane Kennedy was sure that O'Connor's high and
ill-tempered answer to Higginson in 1883 was responsible for
Higginson's doggedness, and when he told Higginson so, the
latter's silence seemed to seal the theory. But this was an
oversimplification, for there were things that Kennedy did not
know. Eldridge, for instance, in writing to Burroughs about the
obituary, says that Higginson had told him his distaste was established early, when he first read Whitman while seasick on a
voyage to the West Indies (Clara Barrus, 1931, p. 302. Eldridge
probably mistakes West Indies for the Azores, for which Higginson sailed a few months after publication of *Leaves of Grass,*
1855). His attitude can be inferred too from Emily Dickinson's
well-known reply to Higginson on April 25, 1862. Obviously
the latter had suspected Whitman of having had a corrupt influence on Emily's poetic form. The discreet Higginson could
not possibly have been recommending the candid Whitman for
the library of a New England maiden he had never seen.

The Higginson story is far too elaborate to be given here
even in outline. Kennedy's assumption may be basically right.
O'Connor certainly knew he himself was making an unusual

attack—even for one so fiery as he. He wrote Whitman that he had gone for the colonel "savagely" and he supposed Higginson's rancor would be roused by the slur on his military conduct at Port Royal. It may be even true that Higginson's afterthought about *Drum-Taps* was originally induced by excessive citation of Whitman's hospital work, a line of defense first introduced by O'Connor in *The Good Gray Poet*.

Whatever the provocation of this attack, the result was serious enough to nettle each and every one of Whitman's close friends, and to evoke defenses from all his sympathetic biographers down to date. To recite the arguments and examine the numerous intricacies is hardly necessary here, for as no one has revived the charge since 1929, it seems effectually laid. One or two of the biographers cite the Quaker element in Whitman's character, and plead the fact that fighting was alien to Whitman's spirit. Such a defense is beside the point which Higginson tried to make: *Drum-Taps* seemed hollow because Whitman called for *all* manner of men to rouse themselves and fight.

John Burroughs was not the first to plead the Quaker element, but he put the case most fully. When he read in 1903 that Higginson had again repeated himself in the Lowell Institute lectures, Burroughs wrote into his journal: "Think of belittling him because he did not enlist as a soldier and carry a musket in the ranks! Could there be anything more shocking and incongruous than Whitman killing people? . . . Whitman was the lover, the healer, the reconciler, and the only thing in character for him to do in the War was what he did do—nurse the wounded and sick soldiers—Union men and Rebels alike, showing no preference. He was not an athlete, or a rough, but a great tender mother-man, to whom the martial spirit was utterly foreign" (Barrus, 339). This is more nearly a diversionary maneuver than a defense. It ignores a whole bundle of biographical facts, and if pressed too far proves embarrassing. Had not Whitman ever since 1846 been martial-minded, both in literal prose and in poetic metaphor?

It may be simpler to say that few people today find any real inconsistency in a man of Whitman's age and temperament urging war and then volunteering to nurse without pay instead of accepting his bounty and fighting for pay. He was about as old as the general officers in the Union Army, and only one of them had a beard so gray. The mass of fighting men were young. We can turn the argument in a direction it has not before taken, and examine some statistics which Col. Higginson himself once gathered for an article on woman suffrage. Here he found that only 60% of Harvard's class of 1861 fought in the Civil War and that among previous graduates the percentage went down steadily until it reached zero for the class of '47. Now if Whitman had gone to Harvard—the condition nearly startles us from our subject!—he would have been in the class of '39 or '40, and he would still have had to wait for seven or eight years before the first few Harvard volunteers would join him ("The Military Argument," *Woman's Journal,* 1884, XV, 59).

Higginson did not mention Lowell, born in the same year with Whitman, who like Whitman had a strain of pacificism but wrote his share of patriotic verse and prose. No one has ever so much as suggested that the abolitionist Lowell should have fought. College sophomores today invariably read in the head-notes to his ode in commemoration of the Harvard men who did serve, that Lowell lost heavily in the war—three nephews. Parallel cases amongst patriotic writers could be kept up for some time, but one more example, better than Lowell's, will suffice. Bayard Taylor, six years younger, did his share by selling some stock to enable a younger brother to fight, and then going off on a writing junket to—Lapland. I have run across none of them, but there are doubtless numerous cases of literary men who could well become the butt of the old political joke on Cleveland, who was wounded in the substitute.

None of this is to say that there was not an occasional man of Whitman's age who did not volunteer. We even have the record of at least one poet of advanced age, H. H. Brownell, who because of his patriotic poems got his chance to fight with Farragut.   The fact that Whitman did not volunteer needed some explanation thirty years ago; today the case for him seems so clear that we can freely quote whatever examples are to be found to the contrary.

MANHATTAN OMNIBUS TO WASHINGTON HOSPITAL

For a period of some four years—from 1859 through 1862—Whitman's way of life seems to have been more or less of a piece, punctuated only by the trip to Boston early in 1860 to publish the third edition, and the opening of the war, which was marked by a diary entry in which he dedicated himself to a pure and wholesome life.   The chief differences after the opening of the war were the nostalgic articles already spoken of and what seems to be, so far as we can tell from surviving records, an increased interest in the street-car and stage drivers.

George Whitman, a brother ten years younger than Walt yet older than the usual recruit, volunteered immediately and served throughout the war.   The Union armies could boast of few soldiers more hardy and faithful or of many who had seen more dust, mud, and blood.   From the Carolinas to Vicksburg, in nearly every state, he marched 12,000 miles in all and fought in twenty-one major engagements.   Nearly all the original regiment had fallen from around him when he was finally captured and had to serve a term in a southern prison camp.   But he survived to march past the onlooking Walt in the Grand Review and, having begun as private, was mustered out major and breveted colonel.   Though there was not so deep a sympathy between Walt and George as between Walt and others of his brothers and sisters, Walt followed George's movements and fortunes with the solicitude of an anxious mother.

The Whitman family one day judged by a newspaper report that George was a casualty at the Fredericksburg debacle.   Thereupon occurred a remarkable change in Walt's way of life, which yet yields its threads of continuity.   For comradeship the sick and wounded soldiers in Washington displaced the Manhattan stage drivers, little hospital notebooks replaced the little street-car notebooks, and for intellectual company Walt thenceforth resorted to what one of them called the "pious" little circle around William Douglas O'Connor instead of to the bohemian writers, actors, and artists who flocked around Henry Clapp.

When Walt got to the Union camp at Falmouth, opposite Fredericksburg, everything was already quiet; he found that George, with only a superficial wound, was still on duty. This was geographically and chronologically the closest Whitman came to actual battle. The general action had occurred six days before his arrival on December 19. He was ten nights in Falmouth, in an officer's tent, busy writing notes both personal and historical. The camp was already well organzed, but the wounded were still dying in field hospital tents; the solemn and nearly anonymous work of burying the dead went steadily on. The poems for *Drum-Taps* henceforward were written in a new mood. In one of them he described them all quite well:

> No poem proud, I, chanting, bring . . .
> But a little book, containing night's darkness, and
> blood-dripping wounds
> And psalms of the dead.
> "LO VICTRESS ON THE PEAKS"

In visiting hospitalized stage drivers in New York, Walt had discovered one Sunday an intense satisfaction in spending the day with a group of convalescent soldiers. So it was that when he returned to Washington, which at the peak contained forty large army hospitals, his part in the war soon became obvious to him. A few hours of work each day at an army paymaster's office gave him the little money that he needed, and allowed him many hours to walk through the hospital wards, supplying the sick and wounded with the little things they wanted, and sitting longer by the cots of those who needed him most.

He very soon began to receive small donations of money to pay for paper, pencils, tobacco, and bits of food he took them. Emerson and his group in Massachusetts contributed regularly, the friends of Walt's family in Brooklyn were a faithful source, and he collected sporadic funds in Washington. The myriads of groups which in the first part of the war offered volunteer services of all sorts had for efficiency been consolidated into two great organizations. Walt while first in Washington allowed himself to be commissioned as an agent of one of these, but he obviously realized almost immediately that this was not the Whitman way of doing things (Item 21, Catalogue of 1955 Detroit Public Library Exhibition from the Feinberg Whitman Collection). He never before had been a joiner, and so early in 1863 he quietly and quickly went his individual way, occasionally reporting on his ministrations in long letters to the New York *Times* and Brooklyn *Eagle*.

He visited many of the hospitals, but the Armory Square, on the Mall near the Smithsonian, became his favorite. It was nearest the dock where many of the wounded were landed. The worst cases, those that couldn't stand the ambulance wagon trip to more remote hospitals, were assigned to Armory. Ward K ultimately began to appear more than any other in his little notebooks which served him the double purpose of a reminder of names and things to do, and a record for use in his newsletters and finally in *Specimen Days* and other reminiscences.

Thus went his life for ten months. He spent November in Brooklyn, economically using every day of a thirty-day railway pass he had obtained at the White House from John Hay, so that he could go home and participate in the local elections. Whitman had grown slowly and surely in his support of the President; the visit to the White House on October 31 showed that his faith was complete. In his diary he wrote: "saw Mr. Lincoln standing, talking with a gentleman, apparently a dear friend. His face & manner ... are inexpressibly sweet—one hand on his friend's shoulder, the other holds his hand. I love the President personally." The diary phrase later became familiar in the language—"the sweetest, wisest soul of all my days and lands."

Walt from December to the following June continued in Washington, except for a visit of about three weeks which he referred to as "Down in the Army at Culpepper and Brandy Station." This trip, made for the purpose of visiting the field hospitals, was possibly of little significance. The army, despite any activity in the New York headlines to the contrary, was in deep-winter camp. Walt left only brief records of the experience.

"First Appearance in the Character of a Man Not Entirely Well"

As summer approached, Whitman began to suffer from a complaint of dizziness. The doctors warned he was overdoing. It was late in June when he gave up and went back to Brooklyn, sick. We cannot agree with Walt when he says that he had before that time enjoyed an unconscious good health or that this was his "first appearance in the character of a man not entirely well." There had been some rather strong hints—if not an actual appearance—of bad health in several preceding years. And his letters to his family show a special care for each symptom. His trouble in June obviously was preliminary to the paralysis which struck him nine years later. His doctor ascribed the illness to work in the hospitals, and during the twenty years of partial paralysis both Walt and his friends repeatedly used this ill health as a main point in their defense against his enemies. Walt's sacrifice proved a telling argument in softening the public mind.

In New York he occasionally visited the hospitals and, as he felt better, resumed some of his old acquaintances among the stage drivers. It was seven months later to a day that he returned to Washington to assume a clerkship in the Indian Bureau of the Department of the Interior, a position obtained through the help of a friend, Assistant Attorney General J. Hubley Ashton.

Again and again Whitman alludes to his having written his war poetry and prose at the time and on the spot. Perhaps because of the sense of immediacy which he wished to lend, he failed to complain of or even acknowledge an ironic fate that dogged him all through the war, especially in his shiftings back and forth between New York and Washington. On the occasions of the early incidents that excited Washington—First and Second Bull Run, the *Monitor* and the *Merrimac*—he was in New York. He then went to Washington where McClellan frequently assured him that all was quiet on the Potomac—and the draft riots occurred in New York. He returned to New York—and the Confederates promptly moved against the capital. He had missed by a fortnight his only chance to hear artillery unlimber for anything better than a salute. In April, 1865, this contrariety, as we shall see shortly, shows an Aeschylean hue.

A New Name—The Good Gray Poet

After eight quiet weeks at work in the Department of the Interior, life began to move very rapidly for Whitman. George was released from prison after anxious months, and Walt went to New York to see him. There *Drum-Taps,* after many tedious delays which he had never complained of, was published. He heard the exciting despatches from the South, then the garbled news from Ford's Theatre. Later, back in Washington he saw the Grand Review, with George in it, and Grant and the new President.

On June 30, quite suddenly, with no forehint at all, came one of the public crises of his life, his discharge by Secretary Harlan.

William Douglas O'Connor was instantaneously indignant. As his wrath gradually shaped itself into words, O'Connor began to see in this rejection by the government the symbol of the rejection by the government's people. Both were equally absurd. Even had Whitman desired to keep still, he could not have done so within the radiant range of O'Connor's hot rhetoric. Ashton's futile attempt to have the poet reinstated probably cleared the way of any objection by Harlan to a new clerkship, without loss of pay, in the Attorney General's office.

O'Connor, with some little help from Whitman, wrote an extended protest, restrained in tone, in the form of a letter addressed to Harlan and designed for the signature of Ashton. Written in O'Connor's beautiful and precise hand on folio pages of great paper, it looks for all the world like a document of state, save for a few insertions in the clear, homely scrawl of Walt Whitman. Obviously it was meant as a kind of public and permanent record, but was for some reason never delivered, so that it remains as a preliminary document—though in different tone—to *The Good Gray Poet.* (This MS. in the Berg Collection will be published elsewhere.)

Whitman was apparently finishing his elegies on Lincoln and the other preparation for the *Sequel to Drum-Taps,* while O'Connor in September was writing *The Good Gray Poet.* By October, Whitman was back in New York to arrange for releasing his *Drum-Taps and Sequel.* On November 4 the first review appeared. O'Connor's defense came out the following January with the imprint of a respected New York publishing house.

And so the war experience ended for Whitman, with that happy phrase "the Good Gray," which was yet a long while in bringing the happy result it finally attained. O'Connor had seen it in Tennyson—"the good gray head which all men know"— and it may already be the most often printed phrase from that popular man's works. Its presence in the three hundred obituaries in the Harned Collection in the Library of Congress is overwhelming evidence of its efficacy at the time of Whitman's death.

The History of Drum-Taps

The first allusion Whitman made to his war poems as a book occurs in a letter to his mother three months after he settled in Washington. "Mother, when you or Jeff writes again, tell me if my papers and MSS. are all right; I should be very sorry indeed if they got scattered, or used up or anything—especially the copy of 'Leaves of Grass' covered in blue paper, and the little MS. book 'Drum-Taps,' and the MS. tied up in the square, spotted (stonepaper) loose covers—I want them all carefully kept" (March 31, 1863).

The blue-covered *Leaves of Grass* was the famous copy, now in the Lion Collection at the New York Public Library, which Harlan examined before he decided to discharge Whitman. The "little MS. book" phrase misled Bucke, who concluded that *Drum-Taps* "had already taken shape in MS."; and a number of biographers since have without justification concluded that, as Bliss Perry puts it, the book was "chiefly composed before the end of 1862." Some of Whitman's MS. books were "little" indeed, and this one may have contained only a few poems, for there is no evidence that Whitman wrote more than a very few early reveille pieces. The MS. package tied up in the loose stonepaper covers was with scarcely a doubt a large one, containing the poems left over from and others written since the 1860 edition—a volume projected before the war, *Banner at Daybreak,* with some reminiscent, instead of expectant, military tones. Some of these poems may already have been adapted and shifted to the *Drum-Taps* collection; certainly several of them ultimately found their way there.

There is, in a conversation between Whitman in his old age and Horace L. Traubel, an implication that a substantial part of *Drum-Taps* was written in Washington. Out of the best paper he would make little notebooks, tying them together, or perhaps getting Nellie O'Connor to stitch them. "I carried sometimes half a dozen such books in my pocket at one time—never was without one of them: I took notes as I went along—often as I sat ... writing while the other fellow told his story. ... I would work in this way when I was out in the crowds, then put the stuff together at home. Drum Taps was all written in that manner—all of it—all put together by fits and starts, on the field, in the hospitals, as I worked with the soldier boys. Some days I was more emotional than others, then I would suffer all the extra horrors of my experience—I would try to write, blind, blind, with my own tears. ... Should I ever get to Washington again I must look up my old cherry tree there—the great old tree under which I used to sit and write, write long, write" (WWC, II, 137).

In Whitman's sessions with Traubel, recollections of his wartime work with the soldiers always affected Walt more deeply than any other memory, and thus in the passage above he is more highly emotional than usual. There is a report or two, however, that Whitman's eyes were occasionally dimmed with tears. Burroughs sometimes saw him come into the store while he was still working on *Drum-Taps,* and write out some note, the tears still diming his eyes (Barrus, 44).

WAR-TIME PUBLISHING

Whitman's desire to get *Drum-Taps* into print was accompanied by an unsuccessful attempt to publish in book form the casual hospital notes which he had melded into newspaper articles and which eventually became the core of *Specimen Days.* An old friend, Redpath, doing a small bit of publishing in Boston, would have done it, but he had no capital, and the idea died.

The publishing of books in 1861, 1862, and 1863 was quite slow. A rough count of all volumes of poetry, including standard American and English reprints published in the northern states, reveals 13, 18, and 21 respectively. There was a sudden jump in 1864 when the number was multiplied two and a half times. From 1864 to 1865 there was an increase from 52 to 63 volumes, a very modest gain for a year which had only three months of war. Book publishing as a whole does not seem to have suffered during the last two years of the war, despite the increased cost of printing which Whitman complained of while arranging for *Drum-Taps.* (*The American Catalogue, 1861-1866* has only

EARLY LINES FOR "LILACS" SHOWING DRASTIC REVISIONS
OF WHITMAN'S CONCEPT OF THE POEM

Courtesy of Charles E. Feinberg

XXVXXV

fragmentary data on books published in the South, but distinctly
southern titles were frequently issued by the best northern houses.)

The publication of war-verse in book form does not seem to
have been profitable to any poet other than Whittier. Melville,
with no reputation as a poet at all, was published by an excellent
firm, but he lost substantially on a book he had to finance himself. Even insignificant poets could obtain a good imprint on
their title pages, while Whitman's book went begging.

Until the very last when the *Sequel* was already printed and
bound into the volume, there is no direct record that Whitman
ever tried to get a publisher for *Drum-Taps*. He actually says a
time or two during the war that he would prefer to handle it
himself. This we can probably interpret as a result of a canny
judgment that he could not obtain a publisher, rather than an
indication he actually wanted none. O'Connor firmly advised
him that his new book deserved the benefits to be derived from
established channels, and he apparently wrote to one Carleton on
the subject (WWC, II, 524).

Two New York Carletons were in the business; Traubel's
index identifies this one as G. W. George W. Carleton was an
author himself and a publisher who brought out six or eight
books during the war. O'Connor possibly thought of him because
two of these volumes were war poetry. Later O'Connor asked
George William Curtis to use his influence to persuade this same
man to bring out *The Good Gray Poet;* still later he expressed
the opinion that Carleton should have nothing to do with *Leaves
of Grass,* but allowed that he would be all right as publisher of
Burroughs' *Notes on Walt Whitman as Poet and Person.* As
a result of his eloquent support of Whitman, O'Connor was for
a while considered for an editorial post on the *Times,* and there
is a hint that Carleton had something to do with the negotiations.
Here the trail to find out just what this man meant to the two
friends runs vaguely out (WWC, I, 86; III, 522). Perhaps
Carleton's name, though not his credit, would eventually have
improved, had he not preferred to bring out in the same month

with *Drum-Taps* a book called *Humbugs of the World* by one Phineas T. Barnum.

Another friend, Trowbridge, tried to find a publisher, whether by Walt's suggestion or merely with his acquiescence the phrasing does not tell us. Trowbridge mentioned the MS. in Boston, where the last edition of *Leaves of Grass* had been published, but he got nowhere, and later reported that Walt's reputation in Boston was unsavory. Such was still the case even after the magnificent defense had done its work. Curtis wrote to O'Connor of *The Good Gray Poet*: "I heard it discussed among the *Dii majores* in Boston, but they do not believe in your poet" (Perry, 175). As Whitman's Boston friends were more influential than his New York admirers, it is not difficult to conclude that he would have as hard time looking for help in Manhattan as in Boston.

A WILL TO PUBLISH

Though we are conditioned to expect admirable qualities to show themselves in Whitman's personality, we are yet astonished at what William James later called his "healthy-mindedness" when we survey the long series of what obviously must have been disappointing setbacks to his desire to have his poems in print. Walt Whitman shows here as a man at man's best. Only by citing chronologically the known references to the book before it was finally published can we appreciate fully the fact that it contains no hint from Walt of bitterness or irony, or even excuse or weariness.

Here they are. May 23, 1863, E. M. Allen to Burroughs: "He has a volume coming out soon called 'Drum Taps' " (Barrus, 5). June 9, to his mother: " . . . if I should succeed in getting a transportation ticket that would take me to New York and back I should be tempted to come home for two or three days, as I want some MSS. and books." (Whitman's published letters cited herein are readily located by date through E. H. and R. S. Miller's *Checklist.*) Nov. 17, to Eldridge, from Brooklyn: "I feel to devote myself more and more to the work of my life, which is making poems. I must bring out Drum Taps. I *must* be continually bringing out poems." Dec. 8, Walt, after returning from Brooklyn, showed the MS to Trowbridge, who reports that it was then nearly ready for publication (*My Own Story,* 381).

February 12, 1864, Trowbridge writes Walt from Massachusetts: "What you write me of yourself and your experiences, interests me, and makes me almost envy you the privilege of being with our noble unfortunate soldiers. You ought to write the epic of this war. By the way, has anything been done with Drum-Taps?"—and he goes ahead to speak of Carleton and of his effort in Boston, already mentioned (WWC, II, 524). March 2, Walt to his mother: "I want to bring out a book of poems, a new one, to be called 'Drum-Taps,' and I want to come to New York for that purpose." March 13, Burroughs to Benton: "Walt is as glorious as ever. ... He expects to bring out his 'Drum Taps' pretty soon. He discoursed with me an hour the other day on his plans and purposes" (Barrus, 18).

April 9, Walt wrote to George Whitman that he hoped to get out his little book that spring (Gohdes and Silver, 167). April 12, Walt to his mother: "I want to come on in a month and try to print my 'Drum-Taps.' I think it may be a success pecuniarily, too." May 25, "I will surely have to come home as soon as this Richmond campaign is decided—then I want to print my new book."

Back in Brooklyn, but by force of illness, July 5, Walt writes O'Connor: "I intend to move heaven & earth to publish my 'Drum-Taps' as soon as I am able to go around" (Berg Collection, unpublished). July 24, in reply to O'Connor, who had sent him "transactions of ironclads, fights &c for '62 & '63—it will probably give me material for some pieces, thumbnail sketches, for my 'Drum-Taps'—I take it you had that in view in sending it to me—I am trying to make arrangements to publish my volume—I shall probably try to bring out myself, stereotype it, & print an edition of 500—I could sell that number by my own exertions in Brooklyn & New York in three weeks"

(Berg Collection, unpublished). August 13, O'Connor to Whitman: "I want very much to hear that Drum Taps are printing." It is in this same letter that O'Connor, as already noted, advises him not to bring out the book himself (WWC, III, 338-9).

September 11, Walt to Nellie O'Connor: "'Drum Taps' is not yet begun to be printed" (Berg Collection, unpublished). Oct. 8, to Eldridge: "My book is not yet being printed. I still wish to stereotype it myself. I could easily still put it in the hands of a proper publisher then and make better terms with him" (Barrus, 20). Dec. 4, to Nellie O'Connor: "About my book nothing particular to tell—I shall print it myself—also my new edition of Leaves of Grass—most likely shall do it in the way we have talked of, namely by subscription—I feel that it is best for me to print my books myself, (notwithstanding some very good objections to that course, but the reasons in favor are far stronger)" (Berg Collection, unpublished).

It was not so very long after July 5 that Whitman was able to go around, and there is no reason not to assume that he did move heaven and earth, but it is obvious he moved no printer to credit him and no publisher to back him. He himself had no money at all; he had gotten to New York on a political railway pass.

Yet Walt, with the same poise, again repeated himself on January 6, 1865, in a letter to O'Connor: "It may be Drum Taps may come out this winter yet (in the way I have mentioned in times past). It is in a state to put right through, a perfect copy being ready for the printer." This time, however, he extended his letter into the fullest critical statement he had made about his own poetry for at least five years. Though it is well known, it is reproduced here: "I feel at last," he wrote, "and for the first time without any demur, that I am satisfied with it—content to have it go to the world verbatim and punctuatim. It is in my opinion superior to Leaves of Grass—certainly more perfect as a work of art, being adjusted in all its proportions and its passion having the indispensable merit that though to the ordinary reader let loose with wildest abandon, the true artist can see that it is yet under control. But I am perhaps mainly satisfied with Drum Taps because it delivers my ambition of the task that has haunted me, namely, to express in a poem (and in the way I like, which is not at all by directly stating it), the pending action of this *Time and Land we swim in,* with all their large conflicting fluctuations of despair and hope, the shiftings, masses, and the whirl and deafening din, (yet over all, as by invisible hand, a definite purport and idea) with the unprecedented anguish of wounded and suffering, the beautiful young men in wholesale death and agony, everything sometimes as if blood-color and dripping blood. The book is therefore unprecedently sad (as these days are, are they not?), but it also has the blast of the trumpet and the drum pounds and whirrs in it, and then an undertone of sweetest comradeship and human love threads its steady thread inside the chaos and is heard at every lull and interstice thereof. Truly also, it has clear notes of faith and triumph.

"Drum Taps has none of the perturbations of Leaves of Grass. I am satisfied with Leaves of Grass (by far the most of it) as expressing what was intended, namely to express by sharp-cut self-assertion, *One's-Self,* and also, or may be, still more, to map out, to throw together for American use, a gigantic embryo or skeleton of Personality, fit for the West, for native models: but there are a few things I shall carefully eliminate in the next issue and a few more I shall considerably change.

"I see I have said I consider Drum taps superior to Leaves of Grass. I probably mean as a piece of art and from the more simple and winning nature of the subject and also because I have in it only, succeeded to my satisfaction in removing all superfluity—verbal superfluity, I mean. I delight to make a poem where I feel clear that not a word but is an indispensable part thereof and of my meaning.

"Still Leaves of Grass is dear to me, always dearest to me as my first-born, as daughter of my life's first hopes, doubts, and the putting in form of those days efforts and aspirations. True, I see now some things in it I should not put in if I were to write now, but yet I shall certainly let them stand, even if but for proofs of phases passed away" (Perry, 150-52).

It was not long after this letter that his first government clerkship finally put Walt in a position where he could pay for printing his book. Actually he contracted for the work before he could have saved enough to pay for it. The timing and nature of the payments recorded below lead rather surely to the conclusion that he actually borrowed money to give his book to the nation, in something like a reverse of the action of Benjamin Franklin when he loaned money to the Congress that was to send him as its ambassador to France. John Burroughs never suggested that he helped finance *Drum-Taps* specifically, but he has told of Walt in those early days of their friendship having frequently borrowed from him, and always punctiliously repaying. We do know that Burroughs loaned him $100 towards the printing of *Leaves of Grass* the following year, and it is quite probable he had been able to help Whitman out before (Barrus, 43). Walt's payment of $20 by mail one day and $14.85 the next suggests that more than one of his friends was called to his aid.

The long record of difficulties, that ended apparently with debt before the sheets were turned over to the binder, lends a kind of richness to the history of a book which after all was not released. Lincoln's death came after most of the first proofs had been pulled. Whitman did not instantaneously recognize that that death was to call forth the great poem of the war, and that he had been preparing himself since long before the war to write it. At the moment he did no more than make a stop-press insertion of a short elegiac poem, "Hush'd Be the Camps To-day." Yet within a week or two, and before it was time to send out review copies, he had obviously realized that the most important delay was yet to come: *Drum-Taps* could not appear without a major Lincoln poem.

In the absence of any recorded hint from Whitman about his reasons for not publishing the book there has been a good deal of surmising, some of it rather careless. Again and again we see statements that the book was "withdrawn," with the frequent conjecture that its failure to sell was one of the reasons. It seems quite obvious, however, that the more frequent assumption that it was withheld because of Lincoln's death is correct. There were no reviews of the book. Anyone slightly familiar with Whitman's promotional activities will conclude immediately that he would not have released it for sale without seeing to it that some sort of notices appeared. I have been able to locate eighteen copies in America, but none of them gives evidence of having been sent out for review.

The broadside Whitman prepared for advertising the volume was printed apparently even before Eckler began the book itself, for there were several changes in the final table of contents. The manuscript for the placard has been reproduced in facsimile in the George M. Williamson catalogue. It is identical with the placard, with two exceptions, only one of which is important. The title of the poem "Flag of stars! thick-sprinkled bunting" was changed on the placard to read "thick-spangled." Both the table of contents and the text in *Drum-Taps,* however, revert to "sprinkled."

On the back of the MS. in the Van Sinderen collection at Yale is written, "Mr. Romes [?] statement: The printed form of this circular was a little larger than the MS. and only about 50 copies were printed for use in the bookstores as placards." The printed form is actually smaller. I know of only three copies of this broadside. The one reproduced in facsimile here, an interesting galley proof with offset from other copies, is now in the collection of Gay Wilson Allen, who has graciously had it copied for me. Mr. Feinberg has a copy; and the third is rarely seen, for Whitman used the back of it for a famous diary note, with the result that it is now pasted face down in the "Lincoln" book at the Library of Congress. This announcement of *Drum-Taps* carries the name of no publisher. While he was overseeing the printing, he must surely have made arrangements with Brooklyn and Manhattan dealers to take consignments of the new book

Walt Whitman's New Volume of Poems.

DRUM TAPS.

To be issued immediately in a small handsome volume, good paper and print. The following is the

TABLE OF CONTENTS:

Drum-Taps.
Song of the Banner at Day-Break.
1861.
The Centenarian's Story.
Pioneers! O Pioneers!
The Dresser.
Rise O Days from your fathomless deeps!
Come up from the fields, father.
Beat! beat! drums!
Vigil strange I kept on the field one night.
A march in the ranks hard-prest and the road un-
known.

As I lay with my head in your lap, camerado.
I dream, I dream, I dream
As toilsome I wander'd Virginia's woods.
As I in vision surfaces piercing.
From Paumanok starting I fly like a bird.
Turn O Libertad.
You foes that in conflict have overcome me.
A soldier returns, he will soon be home.
Quicksand years that whirl me I know not whither.
Over sea hither from Niphon.
Beginning my studies.
When I heard the learn'd astronomer.

Shut not your doors to me, proud libraries.
A sight in camp in the day-break grey and dim.
By the bivouac's fitful flame.
Give me the splendid silent sun.
City of Ships.
Spirit with muttering voice.
Year of meteors.
Years of the unperformed.
A battle, (sights, sounds, &c.)
Angry cloth, I see there leaping.
Flag of stars! thick-spangled bunting.
Lo, the camps of the tents of green.

Aboard at a ship's helm.
Race of weapon'd men.
Out of the rolling ocean, the crowd.
I heard you solemn sweet pipes of the organ.
Cavalry crossing a ford.
Weave in, weave in, my hardy life.
I saw the old General at bay.
World take good notice.
The bivouac halt.
Pensive on her dead gazing.
Reconciliation.
Not youth pertains to me.

Also, will soon be issued, a new edition of

LEAVES OF GRASS,

Entirely revised and much changed from the last edition of 1860-61.

and, having done so, left a copy of the placard. Any withdrawal of the book from the market would then have been only in the sense that he did not deliver the consignment.

Walt's efforts to have his brother George released from a southern war prison were marked by more energy and feeling than Whitman had ever devoted to anything other than writing and publishing. When George was exchanged in March, Whitman went to Brooklyn to see him, and it was this trip that fixed the time in 1865 for printing *Drum-Taps*. Despite the fact he had been at his new government job only eight weeks, he was able to obtain a leave of absence.

New Data from the Feinberg Collection

By Sunday, March 26, Walt had been in New York long enough to see several printers. Their advice that the price of paper and composition would be appreciably lower within a matter of days left him momentarily undecided. The man who had so steadily aspired to be America's poet, who had published volumes in 1855, '56, and '60, had now been silent for five crucial years, and he did not wait the ten days out. On April 1 he entered into a contract with Peter Eckler to stereotype 500 copies for $254.

The details of the printing and binding of both the first edition and later of binding the *Sequel* are contained in numerous receipts and letters which Whitman kept, and which are now part of the collection of Mr. Charles E. Feinberg of Detroit. It is by his courtesy and help that they are reported here, but he is not responsible for error in their interpretation.

Among the other riches in that rich collection is the leather knapsack which became so familiar a sight in the wards of the Washington hospitals; as Walt went down the rows, he drew out of it with unerring tact the right gift to cheer each separate patient. It is not for Mr. Feinberg's help in this volume alone that the dedication honors him, but for his aid also in the study and appreciation of Whitman all over the world, to public

collections and to private scholars alike. Whitman has I believe
been happier in his chief collector than any other poet in history.

The contract in Mr. Feinberg's possession was written out
in Whitman's hand, the provisions actually being contained in a
receipt for a down payment of $63 for three reams of 60-pound
paper. One of its clauses is of interest: "The said book called
'Drum Taps' is to be done on new Long Primer type & make
one hundred & twenty pages, consisting altogether of one hundred
& twenty thousand ems—& the workmanship is to be first class
in every respect & to be completed, & the printed sheets delivered
within one month from this date." It seems, since the book as
printed contained only 72 pages but had roughly the specified
120,000 ems of Long Primer, Whitman had at first settled
on a much smaller page. He wrote to O'Connor on April 7 that
his book would be "small." *Leaves of Grass* had been issued in
8vo, 16mo, and 12mo. Since there is no record of adjustment in
the contract, he apparently intended to try the new size—which
would have been radically different from the large page and print
of his first edition. Possibly he changed his mind after seeing
a sample in galley—and most readers would certainly agree that
his free verse line should not be cramped.

WHITMAN AND THE LINCOLN FUNERAL

Mr. Feinberg has found that the records concerning the
printing and binding reopen, and I believe, resolve with some
degree of satisfaction the puzzled question of where Whitman
spent the first week of public mourning for Lincoln. Every
thread of evidence connecting the country's great democratic president and its democratic poet has been worked over so many times
and has appeared in so many contexts that the general interest of
many and the intense curiosity of some readers has become quite
obvious. A very natural curiosity inheres in the biographical
details behind the composition of the four poems which Whitman
at one stage of *Leaves of Grass* grouped under the general heading "President Lincoln's Burial Hymn."

It has heretofore been assumed that Whitman was back in Washington by the morning of Monday, April 17, and was therefore in the capital where he could have witnessed the sad pageantry of Tuesday, Wednesday, and Thursday, before the funeral train left for the North at dawn Friday, April 21. This assumption has been very natural. Though he had been at work in his new government position only eight weeks, Whitman had managed to get a leave. Moreover he wrote O'Connor on April 7 that his leave had been extended two weeks and that he would return on the 16th or 17th (Sunday or Monday). Presumably his extended leave would terminate Monday morning. It is a natural question whether such a new government clerk, even one treated with the courtesy which Whitman said he had received, could get a second extension running his total leave close to a calendar month.

On May 2, however, Whitman wrote Eckler from Washington: "Before I left New York I paid Bradstreet $20 in advance for binding the first 100" (Rutgers University Library). Mr. Feinberg has a receipt signed by Abraham Simpson of Bradstreet's Bindery and dated April 21 (Friday): "Received of Walt Whitman, Twenty Dollars as advance payment, or part payment, on binding his book, 'Drum-Taps,' according to pattern, etc. at the rate of eighteen cents a volume." This evidence will certainly have to take precedence over the assumption that Whitman would have had to return to Washington to go to work on April 17. It appears definite that he was in New York the very day that the funeral train left Washington for New York.

Also in Mr. Feinberg's collection is a letter from Peter Eckler to Whitman, dated April 22 (Saturday), but the envelope is missing and there is nothing to indicate whether the letter was directed to Brooklyn or Washington except that the phrasing "If I receive an answer" and "you can transmit me the amount" specifically anticipates an answer by mail, and not by person. The indigent poet who had gone to Boston to supervise personally the setting of type for the 1860 *Leaves of Grass* had, we can be

quite sure, hovered over the galley proofs at Eckler's between
April 1 and 15. Consequently the printer, if Walt had been
in Brooklyn, could hardly have assumed that Whitman would
send an answer or transmit a payment. We can see also in
Eckler's phrasing how sternly and characteristically Walt had
disciplined him about following copy: "On page 31 verse 2,
line 3 of DRUM TAPS the word 'recalls' is spelled 'recals'.
According to Webster & Worcester it is wrong but before taking
the responsibility of altering it, I write for your decision. Please
let me know as soon as possible. The other corrections & altera-
tions are made. I enclose a proof of 'O Pioneers' and I think it
is improved. I enclose a bill showing the balance of the account.
If I receive an answer . . . the printing [can be] done by Saturday,
then you can transmit me the amount, and I will deliver sheets
to your binder." Eckler apparently did not enclose the proof for
"O Pioneers," for he crossed out his reference to it. For some
reason the spelling "recal" was allowed to stand until a later
edition.

MATERIAL FOR "LILACS"

These unpublished records of Mr. Feinberg's then begin to
point with considerable accuracy to Whitman's movements on
these days. Sometime during business hours, and after he had
last seen Eckler, Whitman on Friday the 21st visited the bindery
in Manhattan. The next day he was in Washington. He had
perhaps taken an afternoon or evening train, to arrive sometime
during the night.

If this is so, and it seems quite likely, Whitman's consistently
contrary fate to be in New York or Washington at the wrong
time reaches its climax here. He stays in New York too late to
mourn the President in Washington, and leaves New York too
early to be present for the elaborate services there on Monday
and Tuesday. We would like to think that the magnificent
description of the night procession of the funeral train across
the land was a direct transcription of notes taken, as Walt liked,

Hermit Thrush
Solitary Thrush
moderate sized
Prayer from bed

Sings after sundown
sometimes after
in the night
is very beautiful
either standing
near, places

is beautiful —
is very shy

sings in May
& June
not much after
June

is our best
chorister
very clear &
deliberate
a solemn effect

NOTES FOR "LILACS" OBVIOUSLY TAKEN FROM CONVERSATIONS
WITH JOHN BURROUGHS (BARRUS, p. 24)

Courtesy of Charles E. Feinberg

"at the time, and on the spot." Many readers want to believe it possible that Whitman did observe the "pomp of the inloop'd flags, with the cities draped in black",

> With processions long and winding, and the flambeaus of
>   the night,
> With countless torches lit—with the silent sea of faces, and
>   the unbared heads,
> With the waiting depot, the arriving coffin, and the sombre
>   faces.

Yet, search as we might, there is no evidence that Whitman was even allowed the small last privilege of seeing the Lincoln train on his way to Washington. It left Baltimore at three o'clock on Friday afternoon, going to Harrisburg by way of the Northern Central, a road to the west of the one Whitman would take from Philadelphia to Baltimore. The man who was ambitious to "absorb" America apparently had no opportunity to participate in or observe this pageant. Yet he became its chief reporter to the future.

Indirectly, however, he had witnessed it, for the spirit of the land and time was fully represented in New York April 19, the day of the Washington obsequies. I shall elsewhere publish the evidence that he was probably the author of a long article that appeared in the New York *Times* the next day describing the mood of Manhattan and Brooklyn. That day's prose was probably preliminary to the Lincoln hymns.

This revision of our knowledge of Whitman's movements helps explain why he never did allude to the funeral services of the man he mentioned at every opportunity. The following May, in describing the events of the Grand Review, he said nothing in contrast or comparison of it with the solemn procession of thirty thousand people just a month before. He did not mention it in *Specimen Days* nor again later in life in the various addresses he gave on the anniversaries of Lincoln's death. He did not

even allude to it in any way when asked by the *North American
Review* for something he had "not yet described" from his Civil
War relations with Lincoln.

THE PRINTER'S COPY

Only one sheet of printer's copy for *Drum-Taps* has survived.
Now in the collection at Rutgers, it has an endorsement on the
back, in Eckler's hand, indicating it was still in his possession in
1866. I say "printer's copy"—but it was a printer's copy only
in the sense that it was apparently first intended for printer's
copy as indicated by two marks of pagination, one of them in
Whitman's hand—69, or the page on which the poem finally
occurred. O. S. Goad, in the Rutgers Library *Journal*, II, 6-10,
gives a partial facsimile and a complete text showing the various
revisions that are both interlined and pasted on. The final draft
of this MS. differs quite enough from the form of the poem on
its first appearance to warrant the conclusion that Whitman made
yet another fair copy, which he kept with the rest of his printer's
copy of the book, presumably leaving this previous draft at the
printer's shop where he made his revisions. The MS. caption is

Hush'd be the camps to-day.
April 19th 1865.

The subcaption as actually printed reads "A. L. Buried April 19,
1865." The poem contains direct references to the burying of
the body. It was Monday, April 17 that New York papers
announced the plan for burial in the Congressional Cemetery in
Washington. The next day it developed that the chief obsequies
would be in Washington on the 19th, and the body would there-
after be removed to Illinois. It seems then that Whitman either
wrote the poem entirely on Monday, or completed it then, and
that it was probably set up while he was at the shop where he
could read the galley proof. The poem was not reset until 1871,
at which time he changed the date to May 4, the day of interment
in Springfield.

REJECTED LINCOLN ELEGY, PERHAPS CONTEMPORARY WITH
"HUSH'D BE THE CAMPS"

Courtesy of Charles E. Feinberg

Apparently Whitman carried the full printer's copy back to Washington for reference,—else Eckler would hardly have had to inquire about the obvious misprint "recals." Whitman later gave the printer's copy to Peter Doyle, who in 1895 told Bucke: "I once had the manuscript of 'Drum Taps'; Walt made me a present of it. But somehow, when we moved, the manuscript disappeared—was either destroyed or stolen. Part of it was in print, but most of it was written. All his manuscript was pieced together in that fashion" (*Calamus*, 30). We can surmise rather safely that the printed portions of the MS. were the pre-war poems with which he fattened out the slight volume, poems he had had the Rome Brothers print in separate broadsides, as he had frequently done before the war.

Preliminary manuscript drafts of *Drum-Taps* poems are rare. Besides those from the Feinberg Collection reproduced in facsimile here, a few can be cited. Mr. Feinberg has the draft of "O Captain" described by Traubel (WWC, II, 332-3). On the verso of one page of this are found lines 9-14 of "A March in the Ranks Hard-Prest, and the Road Unknown." Lines 15-20 are in the Library of Congress (Item 21, *Walt Whitman, A Catalog*). Charles I. Glicksberg reproduces drafts of other poems in *Walt Whitman and the Civil War*, pp. 121-8.

FEES FOR PRINTING AND BINDING

Peter Eckler obviously received a reply from his letter of April 22, for Mr. Feinberg has a letter from him to Whitman, April 26: "Your book ... will be ready for the Bindery next Monday morning. As there was nothing done yesterday & the day before on account of the funeral, my waiting for your reply did not retard the book. ... Mr. Betts wishes you to send him a copy as soon as published & another copy to Congressional Library in Washington, which will complete your copyright. His office is in Beekman St., in Brinton's Old Theatre." On May 1 Abraham Simpson the binder signed a receipt for the printed sheets, which were thus delivered on the exact date agreed upon a month before (Feinberg Collection).

On May 2 Whitman wrote to Eckler: "I enclose $20 in further liquidation. I wish you would send me a copy of each of the printed sheets, by mail—as I suppose Alvord has printed them. Before I left New York I paid Bradstreet $20 in advance for binding the first 100. I rec'd the copyright & receipt. I thank you for your kindness in getting the copyright" (Rutgers). According to Mr. Feinberg's records, Whitman owed a balance of $34.85 when he sent this letter. On May 3 Whitman wrote again, sending $14.85, "payment in full,"—presumably of the original $254 (Coad, 6). On May 4, obviously after Eckler had received the final payment, he signed over the plates, already in Alvord's possession, as the property of Whitman in the keeping of Alvord.

The original contract called for Eckler to do the presswork, but Whitman presumably knew that the printing was to be sublet to Alvord. Whitman's persistent but frequently thwarted ambition throughout his poetic career was to publish his poems in books which physically were what he termed "first class." Eckler, in signing the receipt written by Walt, had promised the best workmanship "in every respect." Whitman when proposing *Memoranda of a Year* to Redpath (Oct. 21, 1863) specified *"first rate paper,* (this last indispensable)."

Judgment of *Drum-Taps* as an example of book-making, and of the paper it is printed on, I shall have to leave entirely to others, but I can supply a few bits of information. Curtis from his "Easy Chair" spoke of a "plain slight volume" (see Reviews below). Plain it certainly was in comparison to the fanciest thing Scribner had attempted, an anthology published for the Christmas trade that year, *The Book of Rubies,* $10. But it must be noted that Whitman's printer was Alvord, whom Scribner had trusted with his two-color love poems, and who Houghton thought had no superior in this country and few if any in Europe (Editorial, "American vs. English Bookmaking," *Round Table,* Oct. 28, 1865).

What happened to most of the hundred copies Whitman paid in advance to have bound, no one seems to know. Whitman may even have reduced the order to only a few. My census of the known copies, given below, accounts for eighteen, one of them a tied, unbound, uncut copy in the Berg Collection, very probably composed of the sheets which Whitman requested Eckler to send him. William and Nellie O'Connor both had copies (Berg). Whitman may have had the binder send Emerson one, for there was an uninscribed copy in his library.

Whitman's immediate superior, Assistant Secretary of the Interior Otto (WWC, III, 475), as well as Secretary Harlan himself, had a copy of *Drum-Taps*. The only knowledge we have of Harlan's is the comment by O'Connor that there was a copy "in Mr. Harlan's possession" (Bucke, 1883, p. 105). If Whitman presented this to Harlan—the inference seems obvious—he may in doing so have called the Secretary's attention to the fact there was a poet in the Department and thus have set in motion a long series of notable reactions.

Walt possibly handed out a few more copies than are now known, for he inscribed five to unimportant men and women, three of them in 1870, 1871, and 1872. All other copies are without identification. On May 25, in a letter to his mother, Whitman made his only known reference to the disposition of any of the books: "Mother you didn't write whether you got the package of 5 Drum-Taps," but he gave no hint whether he had sent these or had asked the binder to do so.

NEW RECORDS OF THE SEQUEL

The printing of the *Sequel* was not so complicated. Whitman chose enough poems to fill up exactly 24 pages of the duodecimo sheet and had it printed at Gibson Brothers, Washington, the firm which ran the most elaborate colored advertisement in the city directory. The company is still in business in the capital, but its officials can locate no records from Civil War days.

shades of night
heavy
dull — sombre
sombre shades
    " ness
affliction
oppress — oppressive
          " ion
prostration
humble — humility
Suffering — silent suffering
burdensome .
Distress — distressing
Calamity
Extreme anguish, (either of
                    mind or body)
Misery
torture   Calamity
harrassed   Disaster
weighed down   something that strikes
trouble .   down — as by
Deep affliction   Almighty
plaintive

CHARACTERISTIC THESAURUS STAGE OF WHITMAN'S
CATALOGUING METHODS
Courtesy of Charles E. Feinberg

Sorrow (saxon)
grieve
sad
mourn (2usc)
   " ing
   " ful
melancholy
dismal
heavy-hearted
too ?
black
sobs —ing
sighing
funeral rites
wailing
lamenting
mute grief
eloquent silence
bewail
bemoan
deplore
regret deeply
loud lament
pitiful
loud weeping
violent lamentation

anguish
wept sore
depression
pain of mind
passionate regret
afflicted with grief
cast down
downcast
gloomy
serious
sympathy
move compassion
tenderness
tender hearted
full of pity
obscurity
partial } Darkness
or total }
(as the gloom of a
   forest — gloom
   of midnight)
cloudy
cloudiness
   " of mind
mind sunk in gloom
soul " " "
Dejection
dejected

Whitman kept several items, however, which along with the records for *Drum-Taps* are in Mr. Feinberg's collection. On September 20, 1865, Abraham Simpson wrote to Whitman: "When I receive your extra sheet will then bind your 500 'Drum Taps.' Can you give me an order on any person for a copy of your 'Drum Taps' as I want to match them. As I have to pay *nett* cash for the material used in your work would thank you to forward me the money." Simpson's wish here to match the binding of the original issue may indicate that he had bound a considerable quantity—that the hundred copies paid for in advance were actually prepared.

Gibson Brothers on October 2 issued a receipt to Walt Whitman for $50 in payment for 1000 copies of the *Sequel*—composition $24, presswork $4, paper $11.50 and stereotyping $10.50. On October 20, Simpson in New York gave a receipt for $50 paid on account for binding 300 copies. On November 1 he billed Walt for binding 500 copies all told, including the previous 300. Mr. Feinberg has Whitman's personal memo indicating that he sent a copy of *Drum-Taps and Sequel* to the Library of Congress.

When he issued the fourth edition of *Leaves of Grass* in 1867, Whitman apparently had extra sheets of *Drum-Taps* printed from the plates and gathered them, with the 500 *Sequel* sheets remaining unbound, into an undetermined number, but not all, of the copies of that edition.

Had all the sheets been bound, the first issue of *Drum-Taps* would have cost Whitman $254 to Eckler for printing, plus 18c per copy for binding, or 69c each. The book, without mention of the *Sequel*, was listed in *The American Catalogue, 1861-1866* as published by the author at $1, and is incorrectly described as 16mo instead of 12mo. This listing, however it may have gotten into the catalogue, represents some sort of effort on the part of Whitman to sell his book. Since no bookseller could have located and purchased *Drum-Taps* on the sole basis of the catalogue's "N. Y.: The Author," the listing may have resulted from a premature effort similar to the printing of the placard already noted.

The fourth sheet, printed in Washington, brought the total cost of *Drum-Taps and Sequel* to 79c per copy. The marked contrast in the cost of Eckler's and the Gibson Brothers' work is at once obvious. The greatest difference is in the price of paper. The three reams for Eckler cost $63, the two for Gibson, $11.50. An experienced man tells me that the paper for the *Sequel* was apparently chosen to match the first three sheets, and that it is only slightly inferior. Though the printers in New York advised Whitman on March 26 that paper would be much lower in ten days (Allen, 1955, p. 331), the price would scarcely drop 75% in a half year of peace. Therefore we must conjecture that the receipt for $63 may have covered expenses beyond the paper specified. The difference between the two contracts as a whole was not so great, but it was substantial. The two firms provided the same type of services, but Eckler's $254 for 500 copies of three full sheets is about 60% higher than Gibson's $50 for a thousand of one full sheet.

Every book of poems Whitman had so far published was promoted by him with a diligence that leaves its unmistakable marks upon all the larger Whitman collections, for he clipped and kept the notices. The man who got together that extraordinary pamphlet, *Leaves of Grass Imprints,* must certainly have kept clippings of the impression that *Drum-Taps* made. That none of the collections contains even fragments of a clipping notebook suggests the possibility that Whitman kept all the notices well pasted into a well-tied book, which—like O'Connor's scrapbook on *The Good Gray Poet*—has been lost intact and entire.

The absence of all such evidence of his effort to publicize a book he had gone to so much trouble to give the nation is therefore teasing. The only specific record we have of it from Whitman's hand is in a letter to Nellie O'Connor, October 20: "Drum Taps will be bound (a small edition) before you get this—& will next week be put in the hands of a New York publisher & launched on the market,—at least thats [m]y design at pres[ent.]'' Since even this bit of information is from an unpublished letter in the Berg collection, there has heretofore been a void which rather strangely has attracted no comment. Roger Asselineau, deservedly well known for his mastery both of detail and of its interpretation, felt it when he complained that the exact date of publication was hard to determine (*L'Evolution de Walt Whitman,* 166). I had about despaired of learning much about Whitman's efforts to sell his poems, when turning to the advertisement section of *The Round Table* for November 4, 1865, I could not miss at top center a prominently displayed announcement of *Drum-Taps,* "Published this day." *The Round Table* was advertised in the New York *Times* as available November 2.

WHITMAN'S PUBLISHERS BALK

Now the date of publication is helpful to research but of little significance otherwise. The startling thing about this announcement was that it was signed in prominent boldface type by one of the nation's best known publishers, Bunce & Huntington. A note in the personal column of the same issue, apparently written before the advertisement came in, says "we believe" Bunce & Huntington "are to be its publishers."

After the first announcement, the publisher quietly and quickly withdrew—so effectively that Gay Wilson Allen alone has cited any clue that the firm had been interested. The next week a review without the name of a publisher appeared in the same magazine, which was always careful to include publication data. George William Curtis's statement in *Harper's Magazine* as late as December that Bunce & Huntington issued the book was possible because the monthly appeared ahead of date, and copy for the press would ordinarily have had to be ready by November 1. One word—"appalled"—in Curtis's note gives us the hint which we do not need why an established house so promptly bowed out: "a plain slight volume published by Bunce and Huntington, 'Walt Whitman's Drum Taps.' If any reader

is appalled by seeing that name in so choice a society [i.e., Whitman mentioned in the same column with Jean Ingelow and
Tennyson] let us . . . ask if there is no poetry in . . . 'O Captain'
. . . and . . . 'Beat! Beat! Drums!' "

Franklin B. Sanborn, whose review of February 24, 1866,
is cited by Gay Allen, confused the details of publication, but the
general impression is correct. His information would have had
to come from Walt himself, as Allen surmises, or from Burroughs
or O'Connor. No one else knew the details: "he sought in his
native city a publisher for his patriotic verses, but he found none
willing to put his name to the volume. Messrs. Bunce & Huntington finally printed it, but without their name, and without
taking any of the customary steps to introduce the book to the
reading public." Reporting three months after its publication,
Sanborn observes that *Drum-Taps* could scarcely be got at a
bookstore and, though full of the noblest verses, was utterly
unknown to the mass of readers (Allen, 1955, p. 368).

Bunce had advertised it at a dollar, postage paid, twenty-five
cents cheaper than similar patriotic poems in cloth. Whitman
must have given the book over at cost. This price left a margin
of 21 cents for advertising, handling, and postage.

The best book of war lyrics ever written, after the most
tedious delays, first was printed just in time to be withheld.
After another interval, another effort, it gained a publisher. In
less than a week, without a gesture from the district attorney,
he withdrew.

Two weeks after the book was announced, the poetry of
the war passed in review before a large New York audience. On
parade were poems by obscure men along with the great, poems
by men and women, by old and young, by serious and comic
writers. Oliver Wendell Holmes, the lecturer, could hardly
have missed evidences of *Drum-Taps* in the most prominent
literary columns of the day, but he said no word of Whitman
(New York *Times,* Nov. 18; MS. of "The Poetry of the War,"
54 pp., Huntington Library).

; soldiers,
Ashes of *heroes,* blended
with ashes of roses
& lilacs, *fused*
Ashes cerulean *blended with*
the ashes of gray,
Ashes of pine & palmetto
blended,
Ashes of North and South – ashes
of East & West,
Ashes of seaboard & inland
ashes of ~~valle~~ prairie, &
hill & valley rich

A Sacred aroma & ~~powder~~
powder – odor & dust
immortal,

Curious

EXCELLENT BUT REJECTED LINES FOR REVISION OF "HYMN"
(*Drum-Taps*, p. 59) THAT BECAME "ASHES OF SOLDIERS"
IN 1871

Courtesy of Charles E. Feinberg

A kind of anticlimax of misfortunes ends this encouraging story of discouragements. A young man, a friend of Walt's, printed the 1867 *Leaves of Grass* from type. After the remainder sheets of the *Sequel* and perhaps new sheets of the original *Drum-Taps* had been bound in, Whitman, as he later recalled, one day "received intelligence (I was then in Washington) that the place had been seized for debt. I received a portion of the books remaining—the most of them were lost, scattered God knows where, God knows how" (WWC, II, 257). One copy that was not lost was inscribed by Whitman to Albert D. Richardson, now in the Tunstall Collection in the University of Virginia Library. Always interesting and sometimes curious it is to note a poet's own choices of his favorite passages. This copy has Whitman's characteristic blue pencil marks around the chanting catalogue in "A Broadway Pageant" (Facsimile, p. 64, sec. 10).

THE FACSIMILE

The need for a facsimile edition of *Drum-Taps* is obvious. From the section "Drum-Taps" in *Leaves of Grass* as now printed Whitman has dropped numerous poems and added others, and has made so many editorial and textual changes that the original form has been extensively changed. I have found in America 37 copies of the book bound with the *Sequel,* seventeen without the *Sequel.* Many of these have bunched into a few restricted collections open only to highly specialized scholars under conditions unfavorable to prolonged study. In whatever form the original sheets appear, however, and in whatever library, the use is so restricted that it was only through an unusual arrangement the editor of this facsimile was able to obtain a text to work with. *The Poems of Walt Whitman* (New York: Thomas Y. Crowell Company, c. 1902) contained in a later issue a reprint of *Drum-Taps* with the *Sequel,* and a London edition without the *Sequel* was published by Chatto & Windus in 1915. In spite of these, most libraries are without an open-shelf copy. The need for a reading copy for the Whitman lover and for a student's working copy is evident.

It was by a kind of deliberate irony, not altogether free of mischief, that the copies chosen for facsimile come from Massachusetts, where the *Dii majores* of that day "did not like" our poet. Through Carolyn E. Jakeman, the Houghton Library of Harvard University has graciously given permission and has arranged photoduplication of *Drum-Taps* from the library of Amy Lowell, an association copy, and the *Sequel* from the copy previously in Longfellow's library. The Houghton Library will not take amiss the editor's mischief in this conjunction of the Lowell and Longfellow names with Whitman's. Even Thomas Wentworth Higginson finally said he would like to have a Whitman poem, "Joy, Shipmate, Joy!" engraved on his memorial (Mary Thacher Higginson, 1914, p. 395).

A Census of Copies

A census of copies in America, with the significant information concerning them, has been compiled by circularizing the larger libraries and the likely smaller ones. Additional copies were revealed after the census was published in the *Walt Whitman Newsletter* (III, 25-6), and some corrections made possible. According to a marked catalogue in the Lion Collection a pair of books—one with, one without the *Sequel*—was auctioned at Swann's in 1951 for $85. Association copies have brought considerably more.

Drum-Taps, 1865

New York Public Library, Berg Collection, four copies (one was O'Connor's, a second Ellen O'Connor's; a third is a set of tied sheets, unbound and uncut, which I judge are the sheets Whitman requested of Eckler, May 2; the fourth is unidentified); Oscar Lion Collection, one copy (inscribed by Whitman to "Mrs. Johnston")

Harvard, Houghton Library, two copies (one from library of Amy Lowell: "Harry J. Douglas from Walt Whitman November 1872"; one from Emerson's library)

Yale, two copies, Adrian Van Sinderen Collection and Owen F. Aldis gift

University of California Library ("Geo. S. McWatters, from Walt Whitman. Washington Feb. 1870.")

University of Virginia Library, C. Waller Barrett Collection ("Moses Lane—W. W."—possibly not in Whitman's hand)

Boston Public Library

Long Island Historical Society

Historical Society of Pennsylvania

University of Pennsylvania (a copy inscribed to one of Whitman's photographers: "Ernest Denton Seybold from Walt Whitman 1871")

Library of Congress, Carolyn Wells Houghton Collection (The copyright copy has not survived.)

Charles E. Feinberg Collection, two copies

Drum-Taps with *Sequel*

New York Public Library, one copy each in the Berg, Oscar Lion, and Edwin B. Holden Collections

Dartmouth (belonged to P. H. Rumisfin [?] U. S. Army)

University of Virginia Library, C. Waller Barrett Collection, two copies ("Dr T. Sterry Hunt from Walt Whitman" and "C. L. Tartter from Walt Whitman")

Yale, two copies (one copy, rebound, includes "Songs before Parting" and is perhaps an example of a fourth kind of binding combination used by Whitman in 1867)

Detroit Public Library ("J. B. Marvin, from D. A. W." [undoubtedly Wasson] with "friend of Whitman" in another hand beneath Marvin's name)

Library of Congress, three copies (one for copyright; another from H. Buxton Forman's library, "26 August 1869")

Harvard, Houghton Library, two copies (one with signature, "T. B. Aldrich 1865"; one from Longfellow's Library)

Southern Illinois University, from the Feinberg Collection

University of Texas, De Golyer Collection ("Miss Hatty Taylor from 'Papa': February 14, 1866")

Indiana University ("To my friend Arnold Johnson from Walt Whitman—with sincerest ever-loving good wishes.—")

University of Pennsylvania (the 'tall' copy in Harriet Chapman Sprague Collection; see Library of Congress catalogue of her exhibit, p. 10)

Northwestern, Ralph L. Fansler Collection ("Lou Whitman from Walt")

Huntington, two copies

One copy each: Duke, Princeton, Brown, Ohio State universities; Universities of Michigan, Kansas, Minnesota, Chicago; Western Reserve Historical Society, Historical Society of Pennsylvania, Library Company of Philadelphia, Boston Public Library, Newberry Library

Five copies in private collections: Gay Wilson Allen (Traubel's copy, "1892"); Charles E. Feinberg, two copies; Carl Haverlin, New York (Thomas Bird Mosher's copy); Robert D. Faner, Southern Illinois University

The *Sequel* sheet alone, unbound, uncut, but tied (probably Whitman's?) is in the Berg Collection, New York Public Library.

REVIEWS OF DRUM-TAPS

No study or criticism of the poems themselves nor any history of their reception is intended for this volume, which proposes to give only the materials for study. For the convenience of those interested a list of the reviews appears. It must be noted that *The Good Gray Poet* was published in January, 1866, only weeks later; and some readers first saw *Drum-Taps* when it was bound in with the fourth edition of *Leaves of Grass* within twelve months. Contemporary criticism of it cannot be studied entirely apart from these other publications.

Some new material is cited in the following list, but for most of the reviews a partial citation at least is found in W. S. Kennedy's *The Fight of a Book for the World*. One or two of the items I have not been able to locate, so that the accuracy of the citation is not always certain. Burroughs refers to a criticism in the French *Revue de Lundi,* published shortly after *Drum-Taps* (N. Y. *Tribune,* April 13, 1876). The Library of Congress and the Bibliothèque Nationale have no such journal, and none is listed in catalogues of French periodicals. There is no review of that date in the one or two journals which have slightly similar names.

Anon., *Round Table,* [II] (Nov. 4, 1865), 136. (Very slight critical announcement.)

Anon., *Watson's Weekly Art Journal,* IV (Nov. 4, 1865), 34-5.

W. D. H[owells,] *Round Table* [II] (Nov. 11, 1865), 147-8.

[Henry James, Jr.,] *Nation,* I (Nov. 16, 1865), 625-6.

Anon., New York *Times,* November 22, 1865, reprinted in *A Century of Books,* New York Times, 1951. (It is puzzling that this notice could have appeared in the *Times,* unless Whitman's enthusiastic supporter, John Swinton, was absent from the editorial office that week. It could, however, have been the work of Raymond, the man chiefly responsible for founding the *Times* and fixing its temper. Compare his comment cited below.)

[George William Curtis,] in the "Editor's Easy Chair," *Harper's Monthly,* XXXII (Dec. 1865), 123-4.

[Richard Henry Stoddard,] *Round Table,* III (Jan. 20, 1866), 37; Charles Lanham, (Jan. 27, 1866), 61; W. D. O'Connor, (Feb. 3, 1866), 77; Moncure D. Conway, on Whitman in England, (March 17), 171. (Most of these items are more directly concerned with O'Connor's pamphlet.)

"F." *Saturday Press,* Jan. 27 1866, pp. 51-2.

"S." [John James Piatt], Columbus, Ohio, *Morning Journal,* Feb. 12, 1866.

[Franklin B. Sanborn,] Boston *Commonwealth,* Feb. 24, 1866.

[Lord Strangford,] *Pall Mall Gazette,* Feb. 16, 1866. (This was liberally quoted by Conway, whom see above.)

Anon., London *Times,* March 8, 1866.

"B." [Myron B. Benton,] *Radical,* I (April 1866), 311-2.

Anon., *London Review,* June 8, 1866.

Moncure D. Conway, "Walt Whitman," *Fortnightly Review,* VI (Oct. 15, 1866), 538-48.

John Burroughs, "Walt Whitman and His 'Drum-Taps,'" *Galaxy,* II (Dec. 1866), 606-15.

[Henry J. Raymond,] an editor's note, ascribed by Kennedy to Raymond, preceding O'Connor's review of the fourth edition of *Leaves of Grass,* New York *Times,* Dec. 2, 1866, copied in *A Century of Books,* New York Times, 1951.

[Adams Sherman Hill,] *North American Review,* CIV (Jan. 1867), 301-3.

Robert Buchanan, "Walt Whitman," *Broadway Magazine,* November, 1867, pp. 188-95.

Very brief allusions to Whitman are made in the following reviews of books by other authors:

Anon., H. H. Brownell's *War Lyrics, Round Table,* III (Jan. 20, 1866), 34-6.

E. C. S[tedman?,] "Mrs. Howe's Later Lyrics" [includes her war verse], *Round Table,* III (Feb. 3, 1866), 66-7. (Presages Stedman's later favorable criticism of Whitman's metrics.)

[James Russell Lowell,] Howells' *Venetian Life, North American Review,* CIII (Oct. 1866), 610-13.

Perhaps as significant as any of these reviews is a description of *Drum-Taps* written in Whitman's own hand, but in the third person. Moncure D. Conway wrote to O'Connor from England, April 24 [1866], asking him to have Whitman write out an account of himself and his poetry, and suggesting that the information might reach England in time to be inserted in his *Fortnightly* essay on Walt and his works.   A typed copy of this letter in the Berg Collection is accompanied by a sheet containing the following notes in Whitman's hand, apparently for O'Connor's use in replying to Conway at this time, or, less likely, in the later negotiations which led to the English edition of *Leaves of Grass,* sponsored by Rossetti:

"His late production 'Drum Taps' is the expression of the war, the rousing of the North at the commencement, the first losses and defeats, the doubt & terrrible uncertainty, the perseverance, of scenes among the wounded & dying, the smoke & thunder & fierceness of battle—& yet more, all the human interests and sympathies of the struggle.   War itself he does not celebrate."

F. DeWolfe Miller

University of Tennessee
January, 1958

ACKNOWLEDGMENTS

I have already acknowledged the gracious aid of Mr. Charles E. Feinberg of Detroit, and of the Houghton Library of Harvard University. I wish to mention in addition Mr. Feinberg's generosity to the library at the University of Tennessee. Not long after Whitman's death one of the earliest chapters of the Whitman Fellowship was organized at Knoxville, Tenn. It remained the only provincial chapter in the history of that organization, the others having been located in great metropolitan centers. At about that time Charles B. Burke wrote the first dissertation on Whitman. He later became head of the English Department at the University of Tennessee and gave public lectures on Whitman in a day when Walt was not usually assigned reading in college study. We feel grateful to Mr. Feinberg for helping to build upon this past.

Materials in the Henry W. and Albert A. Berg Collection of The New York Public Library have obviously enriched this study of the publication of *Drum-Taps*. Dr. John D. Gordan, curator of the Berg Collection, has been constantly helpful, as has Robert Land of the Manuscript Division of the Library of Congress and John Cook Wyllie, Librarian, University of Virginia. Gay Wilson Allen has provided me with a copy of his very rare galley proof of the *Drum-Taps* placard. The University of Pennsylvania Press has granted permission for quotation from Glicksberg's *Walt Whitman and the Civil War*; Houghton Mifflin, from Bliss Perry's *Walt Whitman*.

Research for this work was supported in part by a grant from the Penrose Fund of the American Philosophical Society. For material aid in preparing this edition I thank the University of Tennessee and Dr. John C. Hodges through whom it came.

Harry J. Douglas,
from Walt Whitman,
November, 1872.

WALT WHITMAN'S

DRUM-TAPS.

New-York.

1865.

CONTENTS.

———

	PAGE
Drum-Taps	5
Shut not your doors to me proud Libraries	8
Cavalry crossing a ford	8
Song of the Banner at Day-Break	9
By the bivouac's fitful flame	16
1861	17
From Paumanok starting I fly like a bird	18
Beginning my studies	18
The Centenarian's Story	19
Pioneers! O Pioneers!	25
Quicksand years that whirl me I know not whither	30
The Dresser	31
When I heard the learn'd Astronomer	34
Rise O Days from your fathomless deeps	35
A child's amaze	37
Beat! beat! drums!	38
Come up from the fields, father	39
City of ships	41
Mother and babe	41
Vigil strange I kept on the field one night	42
Bathed in war's perfume	43
A march in the ranks hard-prest, and the road unknown	44
Long, too long, O land	45
A sight in camp in the day-break grey and dim	46
A farm picture	46
Give me the splendid silent sun	47
Over the carnage rose prophetic a voice	49
Did you ask dulcet rhymes from me?	50
Year of meteors	51
The Torch	52
Years of the unperform'd	53
Year that trembled and reel'd beneath me	54
The Veteran's vision	55
O tan-faced Prairie-boy	56

iv CONTENTS.

Camps of green 57
As toilsome I wander'd Virginia's woods............................. 58
Hymn of dead soldiers 59
The ship 60
A Broadway pageant... 61
Flag of stars, thick-sprinkled bunting 65
Old Ireland................................. 66
Look down fair moon 66
Out of the rolling ocean, the crowd.. 67
World, take good notice... 67
I saw old General at bay................................. 68
Others may praise what they like........ 68
Solid, ironical, rolling orb.............. 68
Hush'd be the camps to-day.. 69
Weave in, weave in, my hardy soul.................... 69
Turn, O Libertad............................... 70
Bivouac on a mountain side.. 70
Pensive on her dead gazing, I heard the mother of all................. 71
Not youth pertains to me.. 72

DRUM-TAPS.

—

1 FIRST, O songs, for a prelude,
Lightly strike on the stretch'd tympanum, pride and joy
        in my city,
How she led the rest to arms — how she gave the cue,
How at once with lithe limbs, unwaiting a moment, she
        sprang ;
(O superb! O Manhattan, my own, my peerless!
O strongest you in the hour of danger, in crisis!   O
        truer than steel!)
How you sprang! how you threw off the costumes of
        peace with indifferent hand ;
How your soft opera-music changed, and the drum and
        fife were heard in their stead ;
How you led to the war, (that shall serve for our pre-
        lude, songs of soldiers,)
How Manhattan drum-taps led.

2 Forty years had I in my city seen soldiers parading ;
Forty years as a pageant — till unawares, the Lady of
        this teeming and turbulent city,
Sleepless, amid her ships, her houses, her incalculable
        wealth,
With her million children around her — suddenly,
At dead of night, at news from the south,
Incens'd, struck with clench'd hand the pavement.

3 A shock electric — the night sustain'd it ;
Till with ominous hum, our hive at day-break, pour'd
        out its myriads.

A*   (5)

4 From the houses then, and the workshops, and
    through all the doorways,
Leapt they tumultuous — and lo! Manhattan arming.

5 To the drum-taps prompt,
The young men falling in and arming;
The mechanics arming, (the trowel, the jack-plane, the
    blacksmith's hammer, tost aside with precipi-
    tation;)
The lawyer leaving his office, and arming — the judge
    leaving the court;
The driver deserting his wagon in the street, jumping
    down, throwing the reins abruptly down on the
    horses' backs;
The salesman leaving the store — the boss, book-keeper,
    porter, all leaving;
Squads gathering everywhere by common consent, and
    arming;
The new recruits, even boys — the old men show them
    how to wear their accoutrements — they buckle
    the straps carefully;
Outdoors arming — indoors arming — the flash of the
    musket-barrels;
The white tents cluster in camps — the arm'd sentries
    around—the sunrise cannon, and again at sunset;
Arm'd regiments arrive every day, pass through the
    city, and embark from the wharves;
(How good they look, as they tramp down to the river,
    sweaty, with their guns on their shoulders!
How I love them! how I could hug them, with their
    brown faces, and their clothes and knapsacks cov-
    er'd with dust!)
The blood of the city up — arm'd! arm'd! the cry
    everywhere;
The flags flung out from the steeples of churches, and
    from all the public buildings and stores;
The tearful parting — the mother kisses her son — the
    son kisses his mother;
(Loth is the mother to part — yet not a word does she
    speak to detain him;)

The tumultuous escort — the ranks of policemen preced-
    ing, clearing the way;
The unpent enthusiasm — the wild cheers of the crowd
    for their favorites;
The artillery — the silent cannons, bright as gold, drawn
    along, rumble lightly over the stones;
(Silent cannons — soon to cease your silence!
Soon, unlimber'd, to begin the red business;)
All the mutter of preparation — all the determin'd
    arming;
The hospital service — the lint, bandages, and medi-
    cines;
The women volunteering for nurses — the work begun
    for, in earnest — no mere parade now;
War! an arm'd race is advancing! — the welcome for
    battle — no turning away;
War! be it weeks, months, or years — an arm'd race is
    advancing to welcome it.

6 Mannahatta a-march! — and it's O to sing it well!
It's O for a manly life in the camp!

7 And the sturdy artillery!
The guns, bright as gold — the work for giants — to
    serve well the guns:
Unlimber them! no more, as the past forty years, for
    salutes for courtesies merely;
Put in something else now besides powder and wadding.

8 And you, Lady of Ships! you Mannahatta!
Old matron of the city! this proud, friendly, turbulent
    city!
Often in peace and wealth you were pensive, or covertly
    frown'd amid all your children;
But now you smile with joy, exulting old Mannahatta!

SHUT NOT YOUR DOORS TO ME PROUD LIBRARIES.

SHUT not your doors to me, proud libraries,
For that which was lacking among you all, yet needed
    most, I bring ;
A book I have made for your dear sake, O soldiers,
And for you, O soul of man, and you, love of comrades ;
The words of my book nothing, the life of it every-
    thing ;
A book separate, not link'd with the rest, nor felt by
    the intellect ;
But you will feel every word, O Libertad ! arm'd
    Libertad !
It shall pass by the intellect to swim the sea, the air,
With joy with you, O soul of man.

CAVALRY CROSSING A FORD.

A LINE in long array, where they wind betwixt green
    islands ;
They take a serpentine course — their arms flash in the
    sun — Hark to the musical clank ;
Behold the silvery river — in it the splashing horses,
    loitering, stop to drink ;
Behold the brown-faced men — each group, each person,
    a picture — the negligent rest on the saddles ;
Some emerge on the opposite bank — others are just
    entering the ford ;
The guidon flags flutter gaily in the wind.

SONG

OF

THE BANNER AT DAY-BREAK.

———

POET.

1 O A new song, a free song,
Flapping, flapping, flapping, flapping, by sounds, by
  voices clearer,
By the wind's voice and that of the drum,
By the banner's voice, and child's voice, and sea's voice,
  and father's voice,
Low on the ground and high in the air,
On the ground where father and child stand,
In the upward air where their eyes turn,
Where the banner at day-break is flapping.

2 Words! book-words! what are you?
Words no more, for hearken and see,
My song is there in the open air — and I must sing,
With the banner and pennant a-flapping.

3 I'll weave the chord and twine in,
Man's desire and babe's desire — I'll twine them in, I'll
  put in life;
I'll put the bayonet's flashing point — I'll let bullets and
  slugs whizz;
I'll pour the verse with streams of blood, full of volition,
  full of joy;
Then loosen, launch forth, to go and compete,
With the banner and pennant a-flapping.

(9)

BANNER AND PENNANT.

4 Come up here, bard, bard; *(Poet)*
Come up here, soul, soul;
Come up here, dear little child,
To fly in the clouds and winds with us, and play with
    the measureless light.

CHILD.

5 Father, what is that in the sky beckoning to me with
    long finger?
And what does it say to me all the while?

FATHER.

6 Nothing, my babe, you see in the sky;
And nothing at all to you it says. But look you, my
    babe,
Look at these dazzling things in the houses, and see you
    the money-shops opening;
And see you the vehicles preparing to crawl along the
    streets with goods:
These! ah, these! how valued and toil'd for, these!
How envied by all the earth!

POET.

7 Fresh and rosy red, the sun is mounting high;
On floats the sea in distant blue, careering through its
    channels;
On floats the wind over the breast of the sea, setting in
    toward land;
The great steady wind from west and west-by-south,
Floating so buoyant, with milk-white foam on the waters.

8 But I am not the sea, nor the red sun;
I am not the wind, with girlish laughter;
Not the immense wind which strengthens — not the
    wind which lashes;
Not the spirit that ever lashes its own body to terror and
    death:

But I am of that which unseen comes and sings, sings,
  sings,
Which babbles in brooks and scoots in showers on the
  land;
Which the birds know in the woods, mornings and
  evenings,
And the shore-sands know, and the hissing wave, and
  that banner and pennant,
Aloft there flapping and flapping.

CHILD.

9 O father, it is alive — it is full of people — it has
  children!
O now it seems to me it is talking to its children!
I hear it — it talks to me — O it is wonderful!
O it stretches — it spreads and runs so fast! O my
  father,
It is so broad, it covers the whole sky!

FATHER.

10 Cease, cease, my foolish babe,
What you are saying is sorrowful to me — much it dis-
  pleases me;
Behold with the rest, again I say — behold not banners
  and pennants aloft;
But the well-prepared pavements behold — and mark
  the solid-wall'd houses.

BANNER AND PENNANT.

11 Speak to the child, O bard, out of Manhattan;
Speak to our children all, or north or south of Manhat-
  tan,
Where our factory-engines hum, where our miners
  delve the ground,
Where our hoarse Niagara rumbles, where our prairie-
  plows are plowing;
Speak, O bard! point this day, leaving all the rest, to
  us over all — and yet we know not why;
For what are we, mere strips of cloth, profiting nothing,
Only flapping in the wind?

POET.

12 I hear and see not strips of cloth alone;
I hear the tramp of armies, I hear the challenging
    sentry;
I hear the jubilant shouts of millions of men — I hear
    LIBERTY!
I hear the drums beat, and the trumpets blowing;
I myself move abroad, swift-rising, flying then;
I use the wings of the land-bird, and use the wings of
    the sea-bird, and look down as from a height;
I do not deny the precious results of peace — I see pop-
    ulous cities, with wealth incalculable;
I see numberless farms — I see the farmers working in
    their fields or barns;
I see mechanics working — I see buildings everywhere
    founded, going up, or finish'd;
I see trains of cars swiftly speeding along railroad
    tracks, drawn by the locomotives;
I see the stores, depots, of Boston, Baltimore, Charles-
    ton, New Orleans;
I see far in the west the immense area of grain — I
    dwell awhile, hovering;
I pass to the lumber forests of the north, and again
    to the southern plantation, and again to Cali-
    fornia;
Sweeping the whole, I see the countless profit, the
    busy gatherings, earned wages;
See the identity formed out of thirty-six spacious and
    haughty States, (and many more to come;)
See forts on the shores of harbors — see ships sailing in
    and out;
Then over all, (aye! aye!) my little and lengthen'd pen-
    nant shaped like a sword,
Runs swiftly up, indicating war and defiance—And now
    the halyards have rais'd it,
Side of my banner broad and blue — side of my starry
    banner,
Discarding peace over all the sea and land.

BANNER AND PENNANT.

13 Yet louder, higher, stronger, bard! yet farther,
    wider cleave!
No longer let our children deem us riches and peace
    alone;
We can be terror and carnage also, and are so now;
Not now are we one of these spacious and haughty
    States, (nor any five, nor ten;)
Nor market nor depot are we, nor money-bank in the
    city;
But these, and all, and the brown and spreading land,
    and the mines below, are ours;
And the shores of the sea are ours, and the rivers great
    and small;
And the fields they moisten are ours, and the crops and
    the fruits are ours;
Bays and channels, and ships sailing in and out, are ours
    — and we over all,
Over the area spread below, the three millions of square
    miles — the capitals,
The thirty-five millions of people — O bard! in life and
    death supreme,
We, even we, from this day flaunt out masterful, high
    up above,
Not for the present alone, for a thousand years, chant-
    ing through you,
This song to the soul of one poor little child.

CHILD.

14 O my father, I like not the houses;
They will never to me be anything — nor do I like
    money;
But to mount up there I would like, O father dear —
    that banner I like;
That pennant I would be, and must be.

FATHER.

15 Child of mine, you fill me with anguish;
To be that pennant would be too fearful;

B

Little you know what it is this day, and henceforth
    forever;
It is to gain nothing, but risk and defy everything;
Forward to stand in front of wars — and O, such wars!
    — what have you to do with them?
With passions of demons, slaughter, premature death?

POET.

16   Demons and death then I sing;
Put in all, aye all, will I — sword-shaped pennant for
    war, and banner so broad and blue,
And a pleasure new and extatic, and the prattled yearn-
    ing of children,
Blent with the sounds of the peaceful land, and the
    liquid wash of the sea;
And the icy cool of the far, far north, with rustling
    cedars and pines;
And the whirr of drums, and the sound of soldiers
    marching, and the hot sun shining south;
And the beach-waves combing over the beach on my
    eastern shore, and my western shore the same;
And all between those shores, and my ever running
    Mississippi, with bends and chutes;
And my Illinois fields, and my Kansas fields, and my
    fields of Missouri;
The CONTINENT — devoting the whole identity, without
    reserving an atom,
Pour in! whelm that which asks, which sings, with all,
    and the yield of all.

BANNER AND PENNANT.

17   Aye all! for ever, for all!
From sea to sea, north and south, east and west,
Fusing and holding, claiming, devouring the whole;
No more with tender lip, nor musical labial sound,
But, out of the night emerging for good, our voice per-
    suasive no more,
Croaking like crows here in the wind.

POET.
(Finale.)

18 My limbs, my veins dilate;
The blood of the world has fill'd me full — my theme is
    clear at last :
— Banner so broad, advancing out of the night, I sing
    you haughty and resolute;
I burst through where I waited long, too long, deafen'd
    and blinded;
My sight, my hearing and tongue, are come to me, (a
    little child taught me;)
I hear from above, O pennant of war, your ironical call
    and demand;
Insensate! insensate! (yet I at any rate chant you,) O
    banner!
Not houses of peace are you, nor any nor all their pros-
    perity, (if need be, you shall have every one of
    those houses to destroy them;
You thought not to destroy those valuable houses, stand-
    ing fast, full of comfort, built with money;
May they stand fast, then? Not an hour, unless you,
    above them and all, stand fast;)
— O banner! not money so precious are you, nor farm
    produce you, nor the material good nutriment,
Nor excellent stores, nor landed on wharves from the
    ships;
Not the superb ships, with sail-power or steam-power,
    fetching and carrying cargoes,
Nor machinery, vehicles, trade, nor revenues, — But
    you, as henceforth I see you,
Running up out of the night, bringing your cluster of
    stars, (ever-enlarging stars;)
Divider of day-break you, cutting the air, touch'd by
    the sun, measuring the sky,
(Passionately seen and yearn'd for by one poor little
    child,
While others remain busy, or smartly talking, forever
    teaching thrift, thrift;)
O you up there! O pennant! where you undulate like
    a snake, hissing so curious,

showing
ones our
deception by
this symbols

Leadale

Out of reach — an idea only — yet furiously fought for,
    risking bloody death — loved by me!
So loved! O you banner leading the day, with stars
    brought from the night!
Valueless, object of eyes, over all and demanding all —
    O banner and pennant!
I too leave the rest — great as it is, it is nothing —
    houses, machines are nothing — I see them not;
I see but you, O warlike pennant. O banner so broad,
    with stripes, I sing you only, *dedicated*
Flapping up there in the wind.   *to war*

Banner
U.S Flag
Idea of
Country of 1776
Strive to keep
the unity

BY THE BIVOUAC'S FITFUL FLAME.

By the bivouac's fitful flame,
A procession winding around me, solemn and sweet and
    slow; — but first I note,
The tents of the sleeping army, the fields' and woods'
    dim outline,
The darkness, lit by spots of kindled fire — the silence;
Like a phantom far or near an occasional figure moving;
The shrubs and trees, (as I left my eyes they seem to be
    stealthily watching me;)
While wind in procession thoughts, O tender and
    wond'rous thoughts,
Of life and death — of home and the past and loved,
    and of those that are far away;
A solemn and slow procession there as I sit on the
    ground,
By the bivouac's fitful flame.

1861.

Arm'd year! year of the struggle!
No dainty rhymes or sentimental love verses for you,
  terrible year!
Not you as some pale poetling, seated at a desk, lisp-
  ing cadenzas piano;
But as a strong man, erect, clothed in blue clothes,
  advancing, carrying a rifle on your shoulder,
With well-gristled body and sunburnt face and hands—
  with a knife in the belt at your side,
As I heard you shouting loud — your sonorous voice
  ringing across the continent;
Your masculine voice, O year, as rising amid the great
  cities,
Amid the men of Manhattan I saw you, as one of the
  workmen, the dwellers in Manhattan;
Or with large steps crossing the prairies out of Illinois
  and Indiana,
Rapidly crossing the West with springy gait, and de-
  scending the Alleghanies;
Or down from the great lakes, or in Pennsylvania, or on
  deck along the Ohio river;
Or southward along the Tennessee or Cumberland rivers,
  or at Chattanooga on the mountain top,
Saw I your gait and saw I your sinewy limbs, clothed
  in blue, bearing weapons, robust year;
Heard your determin'd voice, launch'd forth again and
  again;
Year that suddenly sang by the mouths of the round
  lipp'd cannon,
I repeat you, hurrying, crashing, sad, distracted year.

FROM PAUMANOK STARTING I FLY
LIKE A BIRD.

—

FROM Paumanok starting, I fly like a bird,
Around and around to soar, to sing the idea of all;
To the north betaking myself, to sing there arctic songs,
To Kanada, 'till I absorb Kanada in myself — to Michi-
    gan then,
To Wisconsin, Iowa, Minnesota, to sing their songs,
    (they are inimitable;)
Then to Ohio and Indiana to sing theirs — to Missouri
    and Kansas and Arkansas to sing theirs,
To Tennessee and Kentucky — to the Carolinas and
    Georgia, to sing theirs,
To Texas, and so along up toward California, to roam
    accepted everywhere;
To sing first, (to the tap of the war-drum, if need be,)
The idea of all — of the western world, one and insep-
    arable,
And then the song of each member of These States.

—

BEGINNING MY STUDIES.

—

BEGINNING my studies, the first step pleas'd me so much,
The mere fact, consciousness — these forms — the pow-
    er of motion,
The least insect or animal — the senses — eyesight;
The first step, I say, aw'd me and pleas'd me so much,
I have never gone, and never wish'd to go, any farther,
But stop and loiter all my life, to sing it in extatic songs.

THE

CENTENARIAN'S STORY.

———

1 Give me your hand, old Revolutionary;
The hill-top is nigh — but a few steps, (make room,
        gentlemen;)
Up the path you have follow'd me well, spite of your
        hundred and extra years;
You can walk, old man, though your eyes are almost
        done;
Your faculties serve you, and presently I must have
        them serve me.

2 Rest, while I tell what the crowd around us means;
On the plain below, recruits are drilling and exercising;
There is the camp — one regiment departs to morrow;
Do you hear the officers giving the orders?
Do you hear the clank of the muskets?

3 Why, what comes over you now, old man?
Why do you tremble, and clutch my hand so convul-
        sively?
The troops are but drilling — they are yet surrounded
        with smiles;
Around them at hand, the well drest friends and the
        women;
While splendid and warm the afternoon sun shines
        down;

(19)

Green the midsummer verdure, and fresh blows the dal-
        lying breeze,
O'er proud and peaceful cities, and arm of the sea be-
        tween.

4 But drill and parade are over — they march back to
        quarters ;
Only hear that approval of hands. hear what a clap-
        ping !

5 As wending, the crowds now part and disperse — but
        we, old man,
Not for nothing have I brought you hither — we must
        remain ;
You to speak in your turn, and I to listen and tell.

THE CENTENARIAN.

6   When I clutch'd your hand, it was not with terror ;
But suddenly, pouring about me here, on every side,
And below there where the boys were drilling, and up
        the slopes they ran,
And where tents are pitch'd, and wherever you see,
        south and south-east and south-west,
Over hills, across lowlands, and in the skirts of woods,
And along the shores, in mire (now fill'd over,) came
        again, and suddenly raged,
As eighty-five years a-gone, no mere parade receiv'd
        with applause of friends,
But a battle, which I took part in myself — aye, long ago
        as it is, I took part in it,
Walking then this hill-top, this same ground.

7 Aye, this is the ground ;
My blind eyes, even as I speak, behold it re-peopled
        from graves :
The years recede, pavements and stately houses disap-
        pear :

Rude forts appear again, the old hoop'd guns are
    mounted;
I see the lines of rais'd earth stretching from river to
    bay;
I mark the vista of waters, I mark the uplands and
    slopes:
Here we lay encamp'd — it was this time in summer also.

8 As I talk, I remember all — I remember the Declara-
    tion:
It was read here — the whole army paraded — it was
    read to us here;
By his staff surrounded, the general stood in the mid-
    dle — he held up his unsheath'd sword,
It glitter'd in the sun in full sight of the army.

9 'Twas a bold act then;
The English war ships had just arrived — the king had
    sent them from over the sea;
We could watch down the lower bay where they lay at
    anchor,
And the transports, swarming with soldiers.

10 A few days more, and they landed — and then the
    battle.

11 Twenty thousand were brought against us,
A veteran force, furnish'd with good artillery.

12 I tell not now the whole of the battle;
But one brigade, early in the forenoon, order'd forward
    to engage the red-coats;
Of that brigade I tell, and how steadily it march'd,
And how long and how well it stood, confronting death.

13 Who do you think that was, marching steadily, stern-
    ly confronting death?
It was the brigade of the youngest men, two thousand
    strong.

Rais'd in Virginia and Maryland, and many of them
    known personally to the General.

14 Jauntily forward they went with quick step toward
    Gowanus' waters ;
Till of a sudden, unlook'd for, by defiles through the
    woods, gain'd at night,
The British advancing, wedging in from the east,
    fiercely playing their guns,
That brigade of the youngest was cut off, and at the
    enemy's mercy.

15 The General watch'd them from this hill ;
They made repeated desperate attempts to burst their
    environment ;
Then drew close together, very compact, their flag
    flying in the middle ;
But O from the hills how the cannon were thinning and
    thinning them !

16 It sickens me yet, that slaughter !
I saw the moisture gather in drops on the face of the
    General ;
I saw how he wrung his hands in anguish.

17 Meanwhile the British maneuver'd to draw us out
    for a pitch'd battle ;
But we dared not trust the chances of a pitch'd battle.

18 We fought the fight in detachments ;
Sallying forth, we fought at several points — but in each
    the luck was against us ;
Our foe advancing, steadily getting the best of it, push'd
    us back to the works on this hill ;
Till we turn'd menacing, here, and then he left us.

19 That was the going out of the brigade of the young-
    est men, two thousand strong ;
Few return'd — nearly all remain in Brooklyn.

20 That, and here, my General's first battle;
No women looking on, nor sunshine to bask in — it
    did not conclude with applause;
Nobody clapp'd hands here then.

21 But in darkness, in mist, on the ground, under a
    chill rain,
Wearied that night we lay, foil'd and sullen;
While scornfully laugh'd many an arrogant lord, off
    against us encamp'd,
Quite within hearing, feasting, klinking wine-glasses
    together over their victory.

22 So, dull and damp and another day;
But the night of that, mist lifting, rain ceasing,
Silent as a ghost, while they thought they were sure of
    him, my General retreated.

23 I saw him at the river-side,
Down by the ferry, lit by torches, hastening the embar-
    cation;
My General waited till the soldiers and wounded were
    all pass'd over;
And then, (it was just ere sunrise,) these eyes rested on
    him for the last time.

24 Every one else seem'd fill'd with gloom;
Many no doubt thought of capitulation.

25 But when my General pass'd me,
As he stood in his boat, and look'd toward the coming
    sun,
I saw something different from capitulation.

TERMINUS.

26 Enough — the Centenarian's story ends;
The two, the past and present, have interchanged;
I myself, as connecter, as chansonnier of a great future,
    am now speaking.

27 And is this the ground Washington trod?
And these waters I listlessly daily cross, are these the
waters he cross'd,
As resolute in defeat, as other generals in their proudest
triumphs?

28 It is well — a lesson like that, always comes good :
I must copy the story, and send it eastward and west-
ward ;
I must preserve that look, as it beam'd on you, rivers of
Brooklyn.

29 See! as the annual round returns, the phantoms
return ;
It is the 27th of August, and the British have landed ;
The battle begins, and goes against us—behold! through
the smoke Washington's face ;
The brigade of Virginia and Maryland have march'd
forth to intercept the enemy ;
They are cut off — murderous artillery from the hills
plays upon them ;
Rank after rank falls, while over them silently droops
the flag,
Baptized that day in many a young man's bloody
wounds,
In death, defeat, and sisters', mothers' tears.

30 Ah, hills and slopes of Brooklyn! I perceive you
are more valuable than your owners supposed ;
Ah, river! henceforth you will be illumin'd to me at
sunrise with something besides the sun.

31 Encampments new! in the midst of you stands an
encampment very old ;
Stands forever the camp of the dead brigade.

PIONEERS!

O PIONEERS!

—

1

Come, my tan-faced children,
Follow well in order, get your weapons ready;
Have you your pistols? have you your sharp edged
    axes?
        Pioneers! O pioneers!

2

For we cannot tarry here,
We must march my darlings, we must bear the brunt of
    danger,
We, the youthful sinewy races, all the rest on us depend,
        Pioneers! O pioneers!

3

O you youths, western youths,
So impatient, full of action, full of manly pride and
    friendship,
Plain I see you, western youths, see you tramping with
    the foremost,
        Pioneers! O pioneers!

4

Have the elder races halted?
Do they droop and end their lesson, wearied, over there
    beyond the seas?
We take up the task eternal, and the burden, and the
    lesson,
        Pioneers! O pioneers!

c   (25)

5

All the past we leave behind;
We debouch upon a newer, mightier world, varied
    world;
Fresh and strong the world we seize, world of labor and
    the march,
        Pioneers! O pioneers!

6

We detachments steady throwing,
Down the edges, through the passes, up the mountains
    steep,
Conquering, holding, daring, venturing, as we go, the
    unknown ways,
        Pioneers! O pioneers!

7

We primeval forests felling,
We the rivers stemming, vexing we, and piercing deep
    the mines within;
We the surface broad surveying, and the virgin soil up-
    heaving,
        Pioneers! O pioneers!

8

Colorado men are we,
From the peaks gigantic, from the great sierras and the
    high plateaus,
From the mine and from the gully, from the hunting
    trail we come,
        Pioneers! O pioneers!

9

From Nebraska, from Arkansas,
Central inland race are we, from Missouri, with the con-
    tinental blood intervein'd;
All the hands of comrades clasping, all the Southern, all
    the Northern,
        Pioneers! O pioneers!

10

O resistless, restless race!
O beloved race in all! O my breast aches with tender
love for all!
O I mourn and yet exult — I am rapt with love for all,
Pioneers! O pioneers!

11

Raise the mighty mother mistress,
Waving high the delicate mistress, over all the starry
mistress, (bend your heads all,)
Raise the fang'd and warlike mistress, stern, impassive,
weapon'd mistress,
Pioneers! O pioneers!

12

See, my children, resolute children,
By those swarms upon our rear, we must never yield or
falter,
Ages back in ghostly millions, frowning there behind us
urging,
Pioneers! O pioneers!

13

On and on, the compact ranks,
With accessions ever waiting, with the places of the
dead quickly fill'd,
Through the battle, through defeat, moving yet and
never stopping,
Pioneers! O pioneers!

14

O to die advancing on!
Are there some of us to droop and die? has the hour
come?
Then upon the march we fittest die, soon and sure the
gap is fill'd,
Pioneers! O pioneers!

15

All the pulses of the world,
Falling in, they beat for us, with the western movement
    beat;
Holding single or together, steady moving, to the front,
    all for us,
        Pioneers! O pioneers!

16

Life's involv'd and varied pageants,
All the forms and shows, all the workmen at their
    work,
All the seamen and the landsmen, all the masters with
    their slaves,
        Pioneers! O pioneers!

17

All the hapless silent lovers,
All the prisoners in the prisons, all the righteous and
    the wicked,
All the joyous, all the sorrowing, all the living, all the
    dying,
        Pioneers! O pioneers!

18

I too with my soul and body,
We, a curious trio, picking, wandering on our way,
Through these shores, amid the shadows, with the
    apparitions pressing,
        Pioneers! O pioneers!

19

Lo! the darting bowling orb!
Lo! the brother orbs around! all the clustering suns and
    planets;
All the dazzling days, all the mystic nights with dreams,
        Pioneers! O pioneers!

20

These are of us, they are with us,
All for primal needed work, while the followers there in
    embryo wait behind,
We to-day's procession heading, we the route for travel
    clearing,
        Pioneers! O pioneers!

21

O you daughters of the west!
O you young and elder daughters! O you mothers and
    you wives!
Never must you be divided, in our ranks you move
    united,
        Pioneers! O pioneers!

22

Minstrels latent on the prairies!
(Shrouded bards of other lands! you may sleep — you
    have done your work ;)
Soon I hear you coming warbling, soon you rise and
    tramp amid us,
        Pioneers! O pioneers!

23

Not for delectations sweet ;
Not the cushion and the slipper, not the peaceful and
    the studious ;
Not the riches safe and palling, not for us the tame en-
    joyment,
        Pioneers! O pioneers!

24

Do the feasters gluttonous feast?
Do the corpulent sleepers sleep? have they lock'd and
    bolted doors?
Still be ours the diet hard, and the blanket on the
    ground,
        Pioneers! O pioneers!
            C*

25

Has the night descended?
Was the road of late so toilsome? did we stop discour-
aged, nodding on our way?
Yet a passing hour I yield you, in your tracks to pause
oblivious,
Pioneers! O pioneers!

26

Till with sound of trumpet,
Far, far off the day-break call — hark! how loud and
clear I hear it wind;
Swift! to the head of the army! — swift! spring to
your places,
Pioneers! O pioneers!

QUICKSAND YEARS THAT WHIRL ME I KNOW NOT WHITHER.

QUICKSAND years that whirl me I know not whither,
Your schemes, politics, fail — lines give way — substan-
ces mock and elude me;
Only the theme I sing, the great and strong-possess'd
soul, eludes not;
One's-self, must never give way — that is the final sub-
stance — that out of all is sure;
Out of politics, triumphs, battles, death — what at last
finally remains?
When shows break up, what but One's-Self is sure?

THE DRESSER.

1 An old man bending, I come, among new faces,
Years looking backward, resuming, in answer to chil-
    dren,
Come tell us old man, as from young men and maidens
    that love me ;
Years hence of these scenes, of these furious passions,
    these chances,
Of unsurpass'd heroes, (was one side so brave ? the
    other was equally brave ;)
Now be witness again — paint the mightiest armies of
    earth ;
Of those armies so rapid, so wondrous, what saw you to
    tell us ?
What stays with you latest and deepest ? of curious
    panics,
Of hard-fought engagements, or sieges tremendous,
    what deepest remains ?

2 O maidens and young men I love, and that love me,
What you ask of my days, those the strangest and sud-
    den your talking recals ;
Soldier alert I arrive, after a long march, cover'd with
    sweat and dust ;
In the nick of time I come, plunge in the fight, loudly
    shout in the rush of successful charge ;
Enter the captur'd works . . . . yet lo ! like a swift-
    running river, they fade ;
Pass and are gone, they fade — I dwell not on soldiers'
    perils or soldiers' joys ;
(Both I remember well — many the hardships, few the
    joys, yet I was content.)

(31)

3 But in silence, in dream's projections,
While the world of gain and appearance and mirth goes
on,
So soon what is over forgotten, and waves wash the
imprints off the sand,
In nature's reverie sad, with hinged knees returning, I
enter the doors — (while for you up there,
Whoever you are, follow me without noise, and be of
strong heart.)

4 Bearing the bandages, water and sponge,
Straight and swift to my wounded I go,
Where they lie on the ground, after the battle brought
in ;
Where their priceless blood reddens the grass, the
ground ;
Or to the rows of the hospital tent, or under the roof'd
hospital ;
To the long rows of cots, up and down, each side, I
return ;
To each and all, one after another, I draw near — not
one do I miss ;
An attendant follows, holding a tray — he carries a
refuse pail,
Soon to be fill'd with clotted rags and blood, emptied,
and fill'd again.

5 I onward go, I stop,
With hinged knees and steady hand, to dress wounds ;
I am firm with each — the pangs are sharp, yet unavoid-
able ;
One turns to me his appealing eyes — (poor boy ! I
never knew you,
Yet I think I could not refuse this moment to die for
you, if that would save you.)

6 On, on I go — (open, doors of time ! open, hospital
doors !)

The crush'd head I dress, (poor crazed hand, tear not the
    bandage away ;)
The neck of the cavalry-man, with the bullet through
    and through, I examine;
Hard the breathing rattles, quite glazed already the eye,
    yet life struggles hard;
(Come, sweet death! be persuaded, O beautiful death!
In mercy come quickly.)

7 From the stump of the arm, the amputated hand,
I undo the clotted lint, remove the slough, wash off the
    matter and blood;
Back on his pillow the soldier bends, with curv'd neck,
    and side-falling head;
His eyes are closed, his face is pale, he dares not look on
    the bloody stump,
And has not yet looked on it.

8 I dress a wound in the side, deep, deep;
But a day or two more — for see, the frame all wasted
    and sinking,
And the yellow-blue countenance see.

9 I dress the perforated shoulder, the foot with the bul-
    let wound,
Cleanse the one with a gnawing and putrid gangrene, so
    sickening, so offensive,
While the attendant stands behind aside me, holding
    the tray and pail.

10 I am faithful, I do not give out;
The fractur'd thigh, the knee, the wound in the abdo-
    men,
These and more I dress with impassive hand — (yet
    deep in my breast a fire, a burning flame.)

11 Thus in silence, in dream's projections,
Returning, resuming, I thread my way through the hos-
    pitals;

The hurt and the wounded I pacify with soothing hand,
I sit by the restless all the dark night — some are so
     young;
Some suffer so much — I recall the experience sweet
     and sad;
(Many a soldier's loving arms about this neck have
     cross'd and rested,
Many a soldier's kiss dwells on these bearded lips.)

WHEN I HEARD THE LEARN'D ASTRONOMER.

WHEN I heard the learn'd astronomer;
When the proofs, the figures, were ranged in columns
     before me;
When I was shown the charts and the diagrams, to add,
     divide, and measure them;
When I, sitting, heard the astronomer, where he
     lectured with much applause in the lecture-room,
How soon, unaccountable, I became tired and sick;
Till rising and gliding out, I wander'd off by myself,
In the mystical moist night-air, and from time to time,
Look'd up in perfect silence at the stars.

Rise O Days from your fathomless Deeps.

1

Rise, O days, from your fathomless deeps, till you loftier
    and fiercer sweep!
Long for my soul, hungering gymnastic, I devour'd
    what the earth gave me;
Long I roam'd the woods of the north — long I watch'd
    Niagara pouring;
I travel'd the prairies over, and slept on their breast — I
    cross'd the Nevadas, I cross'd the plateaus;
I ascended the towering rocks along the Pacific, I sail'd
    out to sea;
I sail'd through the storm, I was refresh'd by the storm;
I watch'd with joy the threatening maws of the waves;
I mark'd the white combs where they career'd so high,
    curling over;
I heard the wind piping, I saw the black clouds;
Saw from below what arose and mounted, (O superb! O
    wild as my heart, and powerful!)
Heard the continuous thunder, as it bellow'd after the
    lightning;
Noted the slender and jagged threads of lightning, as
    sudden and fast amid the din they chased each
    other across the sky;
— These, and such as these, I, elate, saw — saw with
    wonder, yet pensive and masterful;
All the menacing might of the globe uprisen around me;
Yet there with my soul I fed — I fed content, super-
    cilious.

(85)

2

'Twas well, O soul! 'twas a good preparation you gave
    me!
Now we advance our latent and ampler hunger to fill;
Now we go forth to receive what the earth and the sea
    never gave us;
Not through the mighty woods we go, but through the
    mightier cities;
Something for us is pouring now, more than Niagara
    pouring;
Torrents of men, (sources and rills of the Northwest, are
    you indeed inexhaustible?)
What, to pavements and homesteads here — what were
    those storms of the mountains and sea?
What, to passions I witness around me to-day? Was
    the sea risen?
Was the wind piping the pipe of death under the black
    clouds?
Lo! from deeps more unfathomable, something more
    deadly and savage;
Manhattan, rising, advancing with menacing front —
    Cincinnati, Chicago, unchain'd;
—What was that swell I saw on the ocean? behold
    what comes here!
How it climbs with daring feet and hands! how it
    dashes!
How the true thunder bellows after the lightning! how
    bright the flashes of lightning!
How DEMOCRACY, with desperate vengeful port strides
    on, shown through the dark by those flashes of
    lightning!
(Yet a mournful wail and low sob I fancied I heard
    through the dark,
In a lull of the deafening confusion.)

3

Thunder on! stride on Democracy! strike with vengeful
    stroke!
And do you rise higher than ever yet, O days, O cities!

Crash heavier, heavier yet, O storms! you have done
    me good;
My soul, prepared in the mountains, absorbs your im-
    mortal strong nutriment;
Long had I walk'd my cities, my country roads, through
    farms, only half satisfied;
One doubt, nauseous, undulating like a snake, crawl'd
    on the ground before me,
Continually preceding my steps, turning upon me oft,
    ironically hissing low;
— The cities I loved so well, I abandon'd and left — I
    sped to the certainties suitable to me;
Hungering, hungering, hungering, for primal energies,
    and Nature's dauntlessness,
I refresh'd myself with it only, I could relish it only;
I waited the bursting forth of the pent fire — on the
    water and air I waited long;
— But now I no longer wait — I am fully satisfied — I
    am glutted;
I have witness'd the true lightning — I have witness'd
    my cities electric;
I have lived to behold man burst forth, and warlike
    America rise;
Hence I will seek no more the food of the northern soli-
    tary wilds,
No more on the mountains roam, or sail the stormy sea.

A CHILD'S AMAZE.

SILENT and amazed, even when a little boy,
I remember I heard the preacher every Sunday put God
    in his statements,
As contending against some being or influence.

BEAT ! BEAT ! DRUMS !

1

BEAT! beat! drums! — Blow! bugles! blow!

Through the windows — through doors — burst like a force of ruthless men,

Into the solemn church, and scatter the congregation;

Into the school where the scholar is studying:

Leave not the bridegroom quiet — no happiness must he have now with his bride;

Nor the peaceful farmer any peace, plowing his field or gathering his grain;

So fierce you whirr and pound, you drums — so shrill you bugles blow.

2

Beat! beat! drums! — Blow! bugles! blow!

Over the traffic of cities — over the rumble of wheels in the streets:

Are beds prepared for sleepers at night in the houses? No sleepers must sleep in those beds;

No bargainers' bargains by day — no brokers or speculators — Would they continue?

Would the talkers be talking? would the singer attempt to sing?

Would the lawyer rise in the court to state his case before the judge?

Then rattle quicker, heavier drums — you bugles wilder blow.

3

Beat! beat! drums! — Blow! bugles! blow!

Make no parley — stop for no expostulation;

Mind not the timid — mind not the weeper or prayer;

Mind not the old man beseeching the young man;

Let not the child's voice be heard, nor the mother's entreaties;

Make even the trestles to shake the dead, where they lie awaiting the hearses,

So strong you thump, O terrible drums — so loud you bugles blow.

COME UP FROM THE FIELDS FATHER.

1 Come up from the fields, father, here's a letter from
      our Pete;
And come to the front door, mother — here's a letter
      from thy dear son.

2 Lo, 'tis autumn;
Lo, where the trees, deeper green, yellower and redder,
Cool and sweeten Ohio's villages, with leaves fluttering
      in the moderate wind;
Where apples ripe in the orchards hang, and grapes on
      the trellis'd vines;
(Smell you the smell of the grapes on the vines?
Smell you the buckwheat, where the bees were lately
      buzzing?)

3 Above all, lo, the sky, so calm, so transparent after
      the rain, and with wondrous clouds;
Below, too, all calm, all vital and beautiful — and the
      farm prospers well.

4 Down in the fields all prospers well;
But now from the fields come, father — come at the
      daughter's call;
And come to the entry, mother — to the front door come,
      right away.

5 Fast as she can she hurries — something ominous —
      her steps trembling;
She does not tarry to smooth her white hair, nor adjust
      her cap.

6 Open the envelope quickly;
O this is not our son's writing, yet his name is sign'd;
O a strange hand writes for our dear son — O stricken
    mother's soul!
All swims before her eyes — flashes with black — she
    catches the main words only;
Sentences broken — *gun-shot wound in the breast, cavalry*
    skirmish, taken to hospital,
At present low, but will soon be better.

7 Ah, now the single figure to me,
Amid all teeming and wealthy Ohio, with all its cities
    and farms,
Sickly white in the face and dull in the head, very faint,
By the jamb of a door leans.

8 *Grieve not so, dear mother,* (the just-grown daughter
    speaks through her sobs;
The little sisters huddle around, speechless and dis-
    may'd;)
See, dearest mother, the letter says Pete will soon be better.

9 Alas, poor boy, he will never be better, (nor may-be
    needs to be better, that brave and simple soul;)
While they stand at home at the door, he is dead already;
The only son is dead.

10 But the mother needs to be better;
She, with thin form, presently drest in black;
By day her meals untouch'd — then at night fitfully
    sleeping, often waking,
In the midnight waking, weeping, longing with one deep
    longing,
O that she might withdraw unnoticed — silent from life,
    escape and withdraw,
To follow, to seek, to be with her dear dead son.

CITY OF SHIPS.

—

City of ships!
(O the black ships! O the fierce ships!
O the beautiful, sharp bow'd steam-ships and sail-ships!)
City of the world! (for all races are here;
All the lands of the earth make contributions here;)
City of the sea! city of hurried and glittering tides!
City whose gleeful tides continually rush or recede,
    whirling in and out, with eddies and foam!
City of wharves and stores! city of tall façades of mar-
    ble and iron!
Proud and passionate city! mettlesome, mad, extrava-
    gant city!
Spring up, O city! not for peace alone, but be indeed
    yourself, warlike!
Fear not! submit to no models but your own, O city!
Behold me! incarnate me, as I have incarnated you!
I have rejected nothing you offer'd me — whom you
    adopted, I have adopted;
Good or bad, I never question you — I love all — I do
    not condemn anything;
I chant and celebrate all that is yours — yet peace no
    more;
In peace I chanted peace, but now the drum of war is
    mine;
War, red war, is my song through your streets, O city!

—

MOTHER AND BABE.

I see the sleeping babe, nestling the breast of its
    mother;
The sleeping mother and babe — hush'd, I study them
    long and long.

D*

VIGIL STRANGE I KEPT ON THE FIELD ONE NIGHT.

Vigil strange I kept on the field one night,
When you, my son and my comrade, dropt at my side
    that day,
One look I but gave, which your dear eyes return'd,
    with a look I shall never forget;
One touch of your hand to mine, O boy, reach'd up as
    you lay on the ground;
Then onward I sped in the battle, the even-contested
    battle;
Till late in the night reliev'd, to the place at last again I
    made my way;
Found you in death so cold, dear comrade — found your
    body, son of responding kisses, (never again on
    earth responding:)
Bared your face in the starlight — curious the scene —
    cool blew the moderate night-wind;
Long there and then in vigil I stood, dimly around me
    the battle-field spreading;
Vigil wondrous and vigil sweet, there in the fragrant
    silent night;
But not a tear fell, not even a long-drawn sigh — Long,
    long I gazed;
Then on the earth partially reclining, sat by your side,
    leaning my chin in my hands;
Passing sweet hours, immortal and mystic hours with
    you. dearest comrade — Not a tear, not a word;
Vigil of silence, love and death — vigil for you, my son
    and my soldier,
As onward silently stars aloft, eastward new ones up-
    ward stole;
Vigil final for you, brave boy, (I could not save you,
    swift was your death,

I faithfully loved you and cared for you living — I think
    we shall surely meet again ;)
Till at latest lingering of the night, indeed just as the
    dawn appear'd,
My comrade I wrapt in his blanket, envelop'd well his
    form,
Folded the blanket well, tucking it carefully over head,
    and carefully under feet ;
And there and then, and bathed by the rising sun, my
    son in his grave, in his rude-dug grave I de-
    posited ;
Ending my vigil strange with that — vigil of night and
    battle-field dim ;
Vigil for boy of responding kisses, (never again on earth
    responding ;)
Vigil for comrade swiftly slain — vigil I never forget,
    how as day brighten'd,
I rose from the chill ground, and folded my soldier well
    in his blanket,
And buried him where he fell.

BATHED IN WAR'S PERFUME.

BATHED in war's perfume — delicate flag !
O to hear you call the sailors and the soldiers ! flag like
    a beautiful woman !
O to hear the tramp, tramp, of a million answering men !
    O the ships they arm with joy !
O to see you leap and beckon from the tall masts of
    ships !
O to see you peering down on the sailors on the decks !
Flag like the eyes of women.

A MARCH IN THE RANKS HARD-PREST,

AND THE ROAD UNKNOWN.

A MARCH in the ranks hard-prest, and the road unknown;
A route through a heavy wood, with muffled steps in the
    darkness;
Our army foil'd with loss severe, and the sullen remnant
    retreating;
Till after midnight glimmer upon us, the lights of a
    dim-lighted building;
We come to an open space in the woods, and halt by the
    dim-lighted building;
'Tis a large old church, at the crossing roads — 'tis now
    an impromptu hospital;
— Entering but for a minute, I see a sight beyond all
    the pictures and poems ever made:
Shadows of deepest, deepest black, just lit by moving
    candles and lamps,
And by one great pitchy torch, stationary, with wild red
    flame, and clouds of smoke;
By these, crowds, groups of forms, vaguely I see, on the
    floor, some in the pews laid down;
At my feet more distinctly, a soldier, a mere lad, in
    danger of bleeding to death, (he is shot in the ab-
    domen;)
I staunch the blood temporarily, (the youngster's face is
    white as a lily;)
Then before I depart I sweep my eyes o'er the scene,
    fain to absorb it all;
Faces, varieties, postures beyond description, most in
    obscurity, some of them dead;
Surgeons operating, attendants holding lights, the smell
    of ether, the odor of blood;

The crowd, O the crowd of the bloody forms of soldiers
— the yard outside also fill'd;
Some on the bare ground, some on planks or stretchers,
some in the death-spasm sweating;
An occasional scream or cry, the doctor's shouted orders
or calls;
The glisten of the little steel instruments catching the
glint of the torches;
These I resume as I chant — I see again the forms, I
smell the odor;
Then hear outside the orders given, *Fall in, my men,
Fall in;*
But first I bend to the dying lad — his eyes open — a
half-smile gives he me;
Then the eyes close, calmly close, and I speed forth to
the darkness,
Resuming, marching, as ever in darkness marching, on
in the ranks,
The unknown road still marching.

LONG, TOO LONG, O LAND.

LONG, too long, O land,
Traveling roads all even and peaceful, you learn'd from
joys and prosperity only;
But now, ah now, to learn from crises of anguish — advancing, grappling with direst fate, and recoiling
not;
And now to conceive, and show to the world, what your
children en-masse really are;
(For who except myself has yet conceived what your
children en-masse really are?)

A SIGHT IN CAMP IN THE DAY-BREAK GREY AND DIM.

—

1 A SIGHT in camp in the day-break grey and dim,
As from my tent I emerge so early, sleepless,
As slow I walk in the cool fresh air, the path near by
    the hospital-tent,
Three forms I see on stretchers lying, brought out there,
    untended lying,
Over each the blanket spread, ample brownish woolen
    blanket,
Grey and heavy blanket, folding, covering all.

2 Curious, I halt, and silent stand;
Then with light fingers I from the face of the nearest,
    the first, just lift the blanket:
Who are you, elderly man so gaunt and grim, with
    well-grey'd hair, and flesh all sunken about the
    eyes?
Who are you, my dear comrade?

3 Then to the second I step — And who are you, my
    child and darling?
Who are you, sweet boy, with cheeks yet blooming?

4 Then to the third — a face nor child, nor old, very
    calm, as of beautiful yellow-white ivory:
Young man, I think I know you — I think this face of
    yours is the face of the Christ himself;
Dead and divine, and brother of all, and here again he
    lies.

———

A FARM PICTURE.

THROUGH the ample open door of the peaceful country
    barn,
A sun-lit pasture field, with cattle and horses feeding.

GIVE ME THE SPLENDID SILENT SUN.

1

GIVE me the splendid silent sun, with all his beams full-
dazzling;
Give me juicy autumnal fruit, ripe and red from the
orchard;
Give me a field where the unmow'd grass grows;
Give me an arbor, give me the trellis'd grape;
Give me fresh corn and wheat — give me serene-moving
animals, teaching content;
Give me nights perfectly quiet, as on high plateaus west
of the Mississippi, and I looking up at the stars;
Give me odorous at sunrise a garden of beautiful flowers,
where I can walk undisturb'd;
Give me for marriage a sweet-breath'd woman, of whom
I should never tire;
Give me a perfect child — give me, away, aside from the
noise of the world, a rural domestic life;
Give me to warble spontaneous songs, reliev'd, recluse
by myself, for my own ears only;
Give me solitude — give me Nature — give me again,
O Nature, your primal sanities!
— These, demanding to have them, (tired with ceaseless
excitement, and rack'd by the war-strife;)
These to procure, incessantly asking, rising in cries from
my heart,
While yet incessantly asking, still I adhere to my city;
Day upon day, and year upon year, O city, walking
your streets,
Where you hold me enchain'd a certain time, refusing
to give me up;
Yet giving to make me glutted, enrich'd of soul — you
give me forever faces;

(O I see what I sought to escape, confronting, reversing
my cries;
I see my own soul trampling down what it ask'd for.)

2

Keep your splendid silent sun ;
Keep your woods, O Nature, and the quiet places by
the woods ;
Keep your fields of clover and timothy, and your corn-
fields and orchards ;
Keep the blossoming buckwheat fields, where the Ninth-
month bees hum ;
Give me faces and streets ! give me these phantoms in-
cessant and endless along the trottoirs !
Give me interminable eyes ! give me women ! give me
comrades and lovers by the thousand !
Let me see new ones every day ! let me hold new ones
by the hand every day !
Give me such shows ! give me the streets of Manhattan !
Give me Broadway, with the soldiers marching — give
me the sound of the trumpets and drums !
(The soldiers in companies or regiments — some, starting
away, flush'd and reckless ;
Some, their time up, returning, with thinn'd ranks —
young, yet very old, worn, marching, noticing
nothing ;)
— Give me the shores and the wharves heavy-fringed
with the black ships !
O such for me ! O an intense life ! O full to repletion,
and varied !
The life of the theatre, bar-room, huge hotel, for me !
The saloon of the steamer ! the crowded excursion for
me ! the torch-light procession !
The dense brigade, bound for the war, with high piled
military wagons following ;
People, endless, streaming, with strong voices, passions,
pageants ;
Manhattan streets, with their powerful throbs, with the
beating drums, as now ;

The endless and noisy chorus, the rustle and clank of
    muskets, (even the sight of the wounded;)
Manhattan crowds with their turbulent musical chorus
    — with varied chorus and light of the sparkling
    eyes;
Manhattan faces and eyes forever for me.

OVER THE CARNAGE ROSE PROPHETIC
A VOICE.

1 OVER the carnage rose prophetic a voice,
Be not dishearten'd — Affection shall solve the problems
    of Freedom yet;
Those who love each other shall become invincible —
    they shall yet make Columbia victorious.

2 Sons of the Mother of All! you shall yet be victo-
    rious!
You shall yet laugh to scorn the attacks of all the re-
    mainder of the earth.

3 No danger shall balk Columbia's lovers;
If need be, a thousand shall sternly immolate themselves
    for one.

4 One from Massachusetts shall be a Missourian's com-
    rade;
From Maine and from hot Carolina, and another an Ore-
    gonese, shall be friends triune,
More precious to each other than all the riches of the
    earth.

E

s To Michigan, Florida perfumes shall tenderly come;
Not the perfumes of flowers, but sweeter, and wafted
     beyond death.

6 It shall be customary in the houses and streets to see
     manly affection;
The most dauntless and rude shall touch face to face
     lightly;
The dependence of Liberty shall be lovers,
The continuance of Equality shall be comrades.

7 These shall tie you and band you stronger than hoops
     of iron;
I, extatic, O partners! O lands! with the love of lovers
     tie you.

8 Were you looking to be held together by the lawyers?
Or by an agreement on a paper? or by arms?
— Nay — nor the world, nor any living thing, will so
     cohere.

DID YOU ASK DULCET RHYMES FROM ME?

—

DID YOU ask dulcet rhymes from me?
Did you find what I sang erewhile so hard to follow,
     to understand?
Why I was not singing erewhile for you to follow, to
     understand — nor am I now;
— What to such as you, anyhow, such a poet as I?
     — therefore leave my works,
And go lull yourself with what you can understand;
For I lull nobody — and you will never understand me.

Year of Meteors.

(1859-60.)

Year of meteors! brooding year!
I would bind in words retrospective, some of your deeds
    and signs;
I would sing your contest for the 19th Presidentiad;
I would sing how an old man, tall, with white hair,
    mounted the scaffold in Virginia;
(I was at hand — silent I stood, with teeth shut close — I
    watch'd;
I stood very near you, old man, when cool and indiffer-
    ent, but trembling with age and your unheal'd
    wounds, you mounted the scaffold;)
I would sing in my copious song your census returns of
    The States,
The tables of population and products — I would sing of
    your ships and their cargoes,
The proud black ships of Manhattan, arriving, some
    fill'd with immigrants, some from the isthmus
    with cargoes of gold;
Songs thereof would I sing — to all that hitherward
    comes would I welcome give;
And you would I sing, fair stripling! welcome to you
    from me, sweet boy of England!
Remember you surging Manhattan's crowds, as you
    passed with your cortege of nobles?
There in the crowds stood I, and singled you out with
    attachment;
I know not why, but I loved you . . . (and so go forth
    little song,
Far over sea speed like an arrow, carrying my love all
    folded,

And find in his palace the youth I love, and drop these
  lines at his feet ;)
— Nor forget I to sing of the wonder, the ship as she
  swam up my bay,
Well-shaped and stately the Great Eastern swam up my
  bay, she was 600 feet long,
Her moving swiftly, surrounded by myriads of small
  craft, I forget not to sing ;
Nor the comet that came unannounced, out of the north,
  flaring in heaven,
Nor the strange huge meteor procession, dazzling and
  clear, shooting over our heads,
(A moment, a moment long, it sail'd its balls of unearth-
  ly light over our heads,
Then departed, dropt in the night, and was gone ;)
— Of such, and fitful as they, I sing — with gleams from
  them would I gleam and patch these chants ;
Your chants, O year all mottled with evil and good !
  year of forebodings ! year of the youth I love !
Year of comets and meteors transient and strange ! — lo !
  even here, one equally transient and strange !
As I flit through you hastily, soon to fall and be gone,
  what is this book,
What am I myself but one of your meteors ?

THE TORCH.

On my northwest coast in the midst of the night, a
  fishermen's group stands watching ;
Out on the lake, expanding before them, others are
  spearing salmon ;
The canoe, a dim and shadowy thing, moves across the
  black water,
Bearing a Torch a-blaze at the prow.

YEARS OF THE UNPERFORM'D.

YEARS of the unperform'd! your horizon rises — I see it
    parting away for more august dramas;
I see not America only — I see not only Liberty's nation,
    but other nations preparing;
I see tremendous entrances and exits — I see new com-
    binations — I see the solidarity of races;
I see that force advancing with irresistible power on the
    world's stage;
(Have the old forces played their parts? are the acts
    suitable to them closed?)
I see Freedom, completely arm'd, and victorious, and
    very haughty, with Law by her side, both issuing
    forth against the idea of caste;
— What historic denouements are these we so rapidly
    approach?
I see men marching and countermarching by swift mil-
    lions;
I see the frontiers and boundaries of the old aristocracies
    broken;
I see the landmarks of European kings removed;
I see this day the People beginning their landmarks, (all
    others give way;)
Never were such sharp questions ask'd as this day;
Never was average man, his soul, more energetic, more
    like a God;
Lo, how he urges and urges, leaving the masses no
    rest;
His daring foot is on land and sea everywhere — he col-
    onizes the Pacific, the archipelagoes;
With the steam-ship, the electric telegraph, the news-
    paper, the wholesale engines of war,
With these, and the world-spreading factories, he inter-
    links all geography, all lands;

E*

— What whispers are these, O lands, running ahead of
      you, passing under the seas ?
Are all nations communing ? is there going to be but
      one heart to the globe ?
Is humanity forming, en-masse ? — for lo ! tyrants trem-
      ble, crowns grow dim :
The earth, restive, confronts a new era, perhaps a gen-
      eral divine war ;
No one knows what will happen next — such portents
      fill the days and nights :
Years prophetical ! the space ahead as I walk, as I vain-
      ly try to pierce it, is full of phantoms ;
Unborn deeds, things soon to be, project their shapes
      around me :
This incredible rush and heat — this strange extactic
      fever of dreams, O years !
Your dreams, O years, how they penetrate through me !
      (I know not whether I sleep or wake !)
The perform'd America and Europe grow dim, retiring
      in shadow behind me,
The unperform'd, more gigantic than ever, advance, ad-
      vance upon me.

YEAR THAT TREMBLED AND REEL'D
BENEATH ME.

YEAR that trembled and reel'd beneath me !
Your summer wind was warm enough — yet the air I
      breathed froze me ;
A thick gloom fell through the sunshine and darken'd
      me ;
Must I change my triumphant songs ? said I to myself ;
Must I indeed learn to chant the cold dirges of the baf-
      fled ?
And sullen hymns of defeat ?

THE VETERAN'S VISION.

WHILE my wife at my side lies slumbering, and the wars
    are over long,
And my head on the pillow rests at home, and the mys-
    tic midnight passes,
And through the stillness, through the dark, I hear, just
    hear, the breath of my infant,
There in the room, as I wake from sleep, this vision
    presses upon me:
The engagement opens there and then, in my busy brain
    unreal;
The skirmishers begin — they crawl cautiously ahead —
    I hear the irregular snap! snap!
I hear the sounds of the different missiles — the short
    t-h-t! t-h-t! of the rifle balls:
I see the shells exploding, leaving small white clouds —
    I hear the great shells shrieking as they pass;
The grape, like the hum and whirr of wind through the
    trees, (quick, tumultuous, now the contest rages!)
All the scenes at the batteries themselves rise in detail
    before me again;
The crashing and smoking — the pride of the men in
    their pieces;
The chief gunner ranges and sights his piece, and selects
    a fuse of the right time;
After firing, I see him lean aside, and look eagerly off
    to note the effect;
— Elsewhere I hear the cry of a regiment charging —
    (the young colonel leads himself this time, with
    brandish'd sword;)
I see the gaps cut by the enemy's volleys, (quickly
    fill'd up — no delay;)
I breathe the suffocating smoke — then the flat clouds
    hover low, concealing all;

Now a strange lull comes for a few seconds, not a shot
    fired on either side;
Then resumed, the chaos louder than ever, with eager
    calls, and orders of officers;
While from some distant part of the field the wind wafts
    to my ears a shout of applause, (some special
    success;)
And ever the sound of the cannon, far or near, (rousing,
    even in dreams, a devilish exultation, and all the
    old mad joy, in the depths of my soul:)
And ever the hastening of infantry shifting positions —
    batteries, cavalry, moving hither and thither;
(The falling, dying, I heed not — the wounded, dripping
    and red, I heed not — some to the rear are hob-
    bling;)
Grime, heat, rush — aid-de-camps galloping by, or on a
    full run;
With the patter of small arms, the warning *s-s-t* of the
    rifles, (these in my vision I hear or see,)
And bombs bursting in air, and at night the vari-color'd
    rockets.

O TAN-FACED PRAIRIE-BOY.

O TAN-FACED prairie-boy!
Before you came to camp, came many a welcome gift;
Praises and presents came, and nourishing food — till at
    last among the recruits,
You came, taciturn, with nothing to give — we but
    look'd on each other,
When lo! more than all the gifts of the world, you
    gave me.

Camps of Green.

1 Not alone our camps of white, O soldiers,
When, as order'd forward, after a long march,
Footsore and weary, soon as the light lessens, we halt
    for the night;
Some of us so fatigued, carrying the gun and knapsack,
    dropping asleep in our tracks;
Others pitching the little tents, and the fires lit up begin
    to sparkle;
Outposts of pickets posted, surrounding, alert through
    the dark,
And a word provided for countersign, careful for safety;
Till to the call of the drummers at daybreak loudly
    beating the drums,
We rise up refresh'd, the night and sleep pass'd over,
    and resume our journey,
Or proceed to battle.

2 Lo! the camps of the tents of green,
Which the days of peace keep filling, and the days of
    war keep filling,
With a mystic army, (is it too order'd forward? is it too
    only halting awhile,
Till night and sleep pass over?)

3 Now in those camps of green — in their tents dotting
    the world;
In the parents, children, husbands, wives, in them —
    in the old and young,
Sleeping under the sunlight, sleeping under the moon-
    light, content and silent there at last,
Behold the mighty bivouac-field, and waiting-camp of
    us and ours and all,

Of our corps and generals all, and the President over the
    corps and generals all,
And of each of us, O soldiers, and of each and all in the
    ranks we fight,
(There without hatred we shall all meet.)

‹ For presently, O soldiers, we too camp in our place
    in the bivouac-camps of green ;
But we need not provide for outposts, nor word for
    the countersign,
Nor drummer to beat the morning drum.

<hr />

As toilsome I wander'd Virginia's
woods.

—

1 As TOILSOME I wander'd Virginia's woods,
To the music of rustling leaves, kick'd by my feet, (for
    'twas autumn,)
I mark'd at the foot of a tree the grave of a soldier ;
Mortally wounded he, and buried on the retreat, (easily
    all could I understand ;)
The halt of a mid-day hour, when up! no time to lose
    — yet this sign left,
On a tablet scrawl'd and nail'd on the tree by the grave,
Bold, cautious, true, and my loving comrade.

2 Long, long I muse, then on my way go wandering ;
Many a changeful season to follow, and many a scene of
    life :
Yet at times through changeful season and scene, abrupt,
    alone, or in the crowded street,
Comes before me the unknown soldier's grave — comes
    the inscription rude in Virginia's woods,
Bold, cautious, true, and my loving comrade.

Hymn of Dead Soldiers.

1 One breath, O my silent soul,
A perfum'd thought — no more I ask, for the sake of all
    dead soldiers.

2 Buglers off in my armies!
At present I ask not you to sound;
Not at the head of my cavalry, all on their spirited
    horses,
With their sabres drawn and glist'ning, and carbines
    clanking by their thighs — (ah, my brave horse-
    men!
My handsome, tan-faced horsemen! what life, what joy
    and pride,
With all the perils, were yours!)

3 Nor you drummers — neither at reveille, at dawn,
Nor the long roll alarming the camp — nor even the
    muffled beat for a burial;
Nothing from you, this time, O drummers, bearing my
    warlike drums.

4 But aside from these, and the crowd's hurrahs, and
    the land's congratulations,
Admitting around me comrades close, unseen by the
    the rest, and voiceless,
I chant this chant of my silent soul, in the name of all
    dead soldiers.

5 Faces so pale, with wondrous eyes, very dear, gather
    closer yet:
Draw close, but speak not.

6 Phantoms, welcome, divine and tender!
Invisible to the rest, henceforth become my compan-
        ions;
Follow me ever! desert me not, while I live.

7 Sweet are the blooming cheeks of the living! sweet
        are the musical voices sounding!
But sweet, ah sweet, are the dead, with their silent eyes.

8 Dearest comrades! all now is over;
But love is not over — and what love, O comrades!
Perfume from battle-fields rising — up from fœtor
        arising.

9 Perfume therefore my chant, O love! immortal Love!
Give me to bathe the memories of all dead soldiers.

10 Perfume all! make all wholesome!
O love! O chant! solve all with the last chemistry.

11 Give me exhaustless — make me a fountain,
That I exhale love from me wherever I go,
For the sake of all dead soldiers.

THE SHIP.

Lo! THE unbounded sea!
On its breast a Ship, spreading all her sails — an ample
        Ship, carrying even her moonsails;
The pennant is flying aloft, as she speeds, she
        speeds so stately — below, emulous waves press
        forward,
They surround the Ship, with shining curving motions,
        and foam.

A Broadway Pageant.

(Reception Japanese Embassy, June 16, 1860.)

1 Over sea, hither from Niphon,
Courteous, the Princes of Asia, swart-cheek'd princes,
First-comers, guests, two-sworded princes,
Lesson-giving princes, leaning back in their open ba-
      rouches, bare-headed, impassive,
This day they ride through Manhattan.

2 Libertad!
I do not know whether others behold what I behold,
In the procession, along with the Princes of Asia, the
      errand-bearers,
Bringing up the rear, hovering above, around, or in the
      ranks marching;
But I will sing you a song of what I behold, Libertad.

3 When million-footed Manhattan, unpent, descends to
      its pavements;
When the thunder-cracking guns arouse me with the
      proud roar I love:
When the round-mouth'd guns, out of the smoke and
      smell I love, spit their salutes;
When the fire-flashing guns have fully alerted me —
      when heaven-clouds canopy my city with a
      delicate thin haze;
When, gorgeous, the countless straight stems, the for-
      ests at the wharves, thicken with colors;
When every ship, richly drest, carries her flag at the
      peak;
When pennants trail, and street-festoons hang from the
      windows;

F   (61)

When Broadway is entirely given up to foot-passengers
    and foot-standers — when the mass is densest;
When the façades of the houses are alive with people —
    when eyes gaze, riveted, tens of thousands at a
    time;
When the guests from the islands advance — when the
    pageant moves forward, visible;
When the summons is made — when the answer that
    waited thousands of years, answers;
I too, arising, answering, descend to the pavements,
    merge with the crowd, and gaze with them.

4 Superb-faced Manhattan!
Comrade Americanos! — to us, then, at last, the Orient
    comes.

5 To us, my city,
Where our tall-topt marble and iron beauties range on
    opposite sides — to walk in the space between,
To-day our Antipodes comes.

6 The Originatress comes,
The land of Paradise — land of the Caucasus — the nest
    of birth,
The nest of languages, the bequeather of poems, the
    race of eld,
Florid with blood, pensive, rapt with musings, hot with
    passion,
Sultry with perfume, with ample and flowing garments,
With sunburnt visage, with intense soul and glittering
    eyes.
The race of Brahma comes!

7 See, my cantabile! these, and more, are flashing to us
    from the procession;
As it moves, changing, a kaleidoscope divine it moves,
    changing, before us.

8 Not the errand-bearing princes, nor the tann'd Japa-
    nee only:

Lithe and silent, the Hindoo appears — the whole Asiatic
    continent itself appears — the Past, the dead,
The murky night-morning of wonder and fable, inscruta-
    ble,
The envelop'd mysteries, the old and unknown hive-
    bees,
The North — the sweltering South — Assyria — the
    Hebrews — the Ancient of ancients,
Vast desolated cities — the gliding Present — all of
    these, and more, are in the pageant-procession.

9 Geography, the world, is in it ;
The Great Sea, the brood of islands, Polynesia, the coast
    beyond ;
The coast you, henceforth, are facing — you Libertad !
    from your Western golden shores ;
The countries there, with their populations — the mil-
    lions en-masse, are curiously here ;
The swarming market places — the temples, with idols
    ranged along the sides, or at the end — bonze,
    brahmin, and lama ;
The mandarin, farmer, merchant, mechanic, and fisher-
    man ;
The singing-girl and the dancing-girl — the ecstatic
    person — the divine Buddha ;
The secluded Emperors — Confucius himself — the
    great poets and heroes — the warriors, the castes,
    all,
Trooping up, crowding from all directions — from the
    Altay mountains,
From Thibet — from the four winding and far-flowing
    rivers of China,
From the Southern peninsulas, and the demi-continental
    islands — from Malaysia ;
These, and whatever belongs to them, palpable, show
    forth to me, and are seiz'd by me,
And I am seiz'd by them, and friendlily held by them,
Till, as here, them all I chant, Libertad ! for themselves
    and for you.

10 For I too, raising my voice, join the ranks of this
     pageant ;
I am the chanter — I chant aloud over the pageant ;
I chant the world on my Western Sea ;
I chant, copious, the islands beyond, thick as stars in
     the sky ;
I chant the new empire, grander than any before — As
     in a vision it comes to me ;
I chant America, the Mistress — I chant a greater su-
     premacy ;
I chant, projected, a thousand blooming cities yet, in
     time, on those groups of sea-islands ;
I chant my sail-ships and steam-ships threading the ar-
     chipelagoes ;
I chant my stars and stripes fluttering in the wind ;
I chant commerce opening, the sleep of ages having
     done its work — races, reborn, refresh'd ;
Lives, works, resumed — The object I know not — but
     the old, the Asiatic, resumed, as it must be
Commencing from this day, surrounded by the world.

11 And you, Libertad of the world !
You shall sit in the middle, well-pois'd, thousands of
     years ;
As to-day, from one side, the Princes of Asia come to
     you ;
As to-morrow, from the other side, the Queen of Eng-
     land sends her eldest son to you.

12 The sign is reversing, the orb is enclosed,
The ring is circled, the journey is done ;
The box-lid is but perceptibly open'd — nevertheless the
     perfume pours copiously out of the whole box.

13 Young Libertad !
With the venerable Asia, the all-mother,
Be considerate with her, now and ever, hot Libertad —
     for you are all ;

Bend your proud neck to the long-off mother, now
  sending messages over the archipelagoes to you ;
Bend your proud neck low for once, young Libertad.

14 Were the children straying westward so long? so
  wide the tramping?
Were the precedent dim ages debouching westward
  from Paradise so long?
Were the centuries steadily footing it that way, all the
  while unknown, for you, for reasons?
They are justified — they are accomplish'd — they shall
  now be turn'd the other way also, to travel toward you thence ;
They shall now also march obediently eastward, for
  your sake, Libertad.

--~~~----

FLAG OF STARS, THICK-SPRINKLED
BUNTING.

FLAG of stars! thick-sprinkled bunting!
Long yet your road, fateful flag! — long yet your road,
  and lined with bloody death!
For the prize I see at issue, at last is the world!
All its ships and shores I see, interwoven with your
  threads, greedy banner!
— Dream'd again the flags of kings, highest borne, to
  flaunt unrivall'd?
O hasten, flag of man! O with sure and steady step,
  passing highest flags of kings,
Walk supreme to the heavens, mighty symbol — run up
  above them all,
Flag of stars! thick sprinkled bunting!

F*

OLD IRELAND.

1 FAR hence, amid an isle of wondrous beauty,
Crouching over a grave, an ancient sorrowful mother,
Once a queen — now lean and tatter'd, seated on the
    ground,
Her old white hair drooping dishevel'd round her shoul-
    ·ders :
At her feet fallen an unused royal harp,
Long silent — she too long silent — mourning her shroud-
    ed hope and heir ;
Of all the earth her heart most full of sorrow, because
    most full of love.

2 Yet a word, ancient mother ;
You need crouch there no longer on the cold ground,
    with forehead between your knees ;
O you need not sit there, veil'd in your old white
    hair, so dishevel'd :
For know you, the one you mourn is not in that grave ;
It was an illusion — the heir, the son you love, was not
    really dead ;
The Lord is not dead — he is risen again, young and
    strong, in another country :
Even while you wept there by your fallen harp, by the
    grave,
What you wept for, was translated, pass'd from the
    grave,
The winds favor'd, and the sea sail'd it,
And now with rosy and new blood,
Moves to-day in a new country.

LOOK DOWN FAIR MOON.

LOOK down, fair moon, and bathe this scene ;
Pour softly down night's nimbus floods, on faces ghast-
    ly, swollen, purple ;
On the dead, on their backs, with their arms toss'd wide,
Pour down your unstinted nimbus, sacred moon.

Out of the Rolling Ocean, the Crowd.

1

Out of the rolling ocean, the crowd, came a drop gently
    to me,
Whispering, *I love you, before long I die,*
I have travel'd a long way, merely to look on you, to touch you,
For I could not die till I once look'd on you,
For I fear'd I might afterward lose you.

2

(Now we have met, we have look'd, we are safe;
Return in peace to the ocean my love;
I too am part of that ocean, my love — we are not so
    much separated;
Behold the great rondure — the cohesion of all, how per-
    fect!
But as for me, for you, the irresistible sea is to separ-
    ate us,
As for an hour carrying us diverse — yet cannot carry
    us diverse for ever;
Be not impatient — a little space — know you, I salute
    the air, the ocean and the land,
Every day, at sundown, for your dear sake, my love.)

WORLD, TAKE GOOD NOTICE.

World, take good notice, silver stars fading,
Milky hue ript, weft of white detaching,
Coals thirty-six, baleful and burning,
Scarlet, significant, hands off warning,
Now and henceforth flaunt from these shores.

I SAW OLD GENERAL AT BAY.

I saw old General at bay;
(Old as he was, his grey eyes yet shone out in battle
like stars;)
His small force was now completely hemmed in, in his
works;
He call'd for volunteers to run the enemy's lines — a
desperate emergency;
I saw a hundred and more step forth from the ranks —
but two or three were selected;
I saw them receive their orders aside — they listen'd
with care — the adjutant was very grave;
I saw them depart with cheerfulness, freely risking their
lives.

OTHERS MAY PRAISE WHAT THEY LIKE.

Others may praise what they like;
But I, from the banks of the running Missouri, praise
nothing, in art, or aught else,
Till it has breathed well the atmosphere of this river —
also the western prairie-scent,
And fully exudes it again.

SOLID, IRONICAL, ROLLING ORB.

Solid, ironical, rolling orb!
Master of all, and matter of fact! — at last I accept your
terms;
Bringing to practical, vulgar tests, of all my ideal
dreams,
And of me, as lover and hero.

HUSH'D BE THE CAMPS TO-DAY.

A. L. BURIED APRIL 19, 1865.

1 HUSH'D be the camps to-day ;
And, soldiers, let us drape our war-worn weapons ;
And each, with musing soul retire, to celebrate,
Our dear commander's death.

2 No more for him life's stormy conflicts ;
Nor victory, nor defeat — No more time's dark events,
Charging like ceaseless clouds across the sky.

3 But sing, poet, in our name ;
Sing of the love we bore him — because you, dweller in
    camps, know it truly.

4 Sing, to the lower'd coffin there ;
Sing, with the shovel'd clods that fill the grave — a
    verse,
For the heavy hearts of soldiers.

WEAVE IN, WEAVE IN, MY HARDY LIFE.

WEAVE in ! weave in, my hardy life !
Weave, weave a soldier strong and full, for great cam-
    paigns to come ;
Weave in red blood ! weave sinews in, like ropes ! the
    senses, sight weave in !
Weave lasting sure ! weave day and night the weft, the
    warp ! incessant weave ! tire not !
(We know not what the use, O life ! nor know the aim,
    the end — nor really aught we know ;
But know the work, the need goes on, and shall go
    on — the death-envelop'd march of peace as well
    as war, goes on ;)
For great campaigns of peace the same, the wiry
    threads to weave ;
We know not why or what, yet weave, forever weave.

TURN O LIBERTAD.

TURN, O Libertad, no more doubting;
Turn from lands retrospective, recording proofs of the
    past;
From the singers that sing the trailing glories of the
    past;
From the chants of the feudal world — the triumphs of
    kings, slavery, caste;
Turn to the world, the triumphs reserv'd and to come —
    give up that backward world;
Leave to the singers of hitherto — give them the trailing
    past:
But what remains, remains for singers for you — wars
    to come are for you;
(Lo! how the wars of the past have duly inured to you
    — and the wars of the present shall also inure:)
— Then turn, and be not alarm'd, O Libertad — turn
    your undying face,
To where the future, greater than all the past,
Is swiftly, surely preparing for you.

BIVOUAC ON A MOUNTAIN SIDE.

I SEE before me now, a traveling army halting;
Below, a fertile valley spread, with barns, and the orch-
    ards of summer;
Behind, the terraced sides of a mountain, abrupt in
    places, rising high;
Broken, with rocks, with clinging cedars, with tall
    shapes, dingily seen;
The numerous camp-fires scatter'd near and far, some
    away up on the mountain;
The shadowy forms of men and horses, looming, large-
    sized, flickering;
And over all, the sky — the sky! far, far out of reach,
    studded with the eternal stars.

PENSIVE ON HER DEAD GAZING, I HEARD THE MOTHER OF ALL.

PENSIVE, on her dead gazing, I heard the Mother of All,
Desperate, on the torn bodies, on the forms covering the
    battle-fields gazing;
As she call'd to her earth with mournful voice while she
    stalk'd:
Absorb them well, O my earth, she cried — I charge you,
    lose not my sons! lose not an atom;
And you streams, absorb them well, taking their dear
    blood;
And you local spots, and you airs that swim above
    lightly,
And all you essences of soil and growth — and you, O
    my rivers' depths;
And you mountain sides — and the woods where my
    dear children's blood, trickling, redden'd;
And you trees, down in your roots, to bequeath to all
    future trees,
My dead absorb — my young men's beautiful bodies ab-
    sorb — and their precious, precious, precious
    blood;
Which holding in trust for me, faithfully back again give
    me, many a year hence,
In unseen essence and odor of surface and grass, centu-
    ries hence;
In blowing airs from the fields, back again give me my
    darlings — give my immortal heroes;
Exhale me them centuries hence — breathe me their
    breath — let not an atom be lost;
O years and graves! O air and soil! O my dead, an
    aroma sweet!
Exhale them perennial, sweet death, years, centuries
    hence.

NOT YOUTH PERTAINS TO ME.

Nor youth pertains to me,
Nor delicatesse — I cannot beguile the time with talk ;
Awkward in the parlor, neither a dancer nor elegant ;
In the learn'd coterie sitting constrain'd and still — for
    learning inures not to me ;
Beauty, knowledge, fortune, inure not to me — yet
    there are two things inure to me :
I have nourish'd the wounded, and sooth'd many a
    dying soldier ;
And at intervals I have strung together a few songs,
Fit for war, and the life of the camp.

FINIS.

SEQUEL TO DRUM-TAPS.

(SINCE THE PRECEDING CAME FROM THE PRESS.)

~~~~~~

WHEN LILACS LAST IN THE DOOR-YARD BLOOM'D,

AND OTHER PIECES.

~~~~~~

WASHINGTON.

1865-6.

CONTENTS.

	PAGE.
When Lilacs last in the door-yard bloom d	3
Race of Veterans	12
O Captain! my Captain!	13
Spirit whose work is done	14
Chanting the Square Deific	15
I heard you, solemn sweet pipes of the Organ	17
Not my Enemies ever invade me	17
O me! O life!	18
Ah poverties, wincings, and sulky retreats	18
As I lay with my head in your lap, Camerado	19
This day, O Soul	19
In clouds descending, in midnight sleep	20
An Army on the march	20
Dirge for Two Veterans	21
How solemn, as one by one	22
Lo! Victress on the Peaks!	23
Reconciliation	23
To the leaven'd Soil they trod	24

GIBSON BROTHERS, PRINTERS.

When Lilacs Last in the Door-Yard Bloom'd.

~~~~~~

1

1 When lilacs last in the door-yard bloom'd,
And the great star early droop'd in the western sky in the
    night,
I mourn'd ... and yet shall mourn with ever-returning
    spring.

2 O ever-returning spring! trinity sure to me you bring;
Lilac blooming perennial, and drooping star in the west,
And thought of him I love.

2

3 O powerful, western, fallen star!
O shades of night! O moody, tearful night!
O great star disappear'd! O the black murk that hides the
    star!
O cruel hands that hold me powerless! O helpless soul of
    me!
O harsh surrounding cloud that will not free my soul!

3

4 In the door-yard fronting an old farm-house, near the
    white-wash'd palings;
Stands the lilac bush, tall-growing, with heart-shaped leaves
    of rich green,
With many a pointed blossom, rising, delicate, with the
    perfume strong I love,

With every leaf a miracle ...... and from this bush in the
     door-yard,
With its delicate-color'd blossoms, and heart-shaped leaves
     of rich green,
A sprig, with its flower, I break.

4

5 In the swamp, in secluded recesses,
A shy and hidden bird is warbling a song.

6 Solitary, the thrush,
The hermit, withdrawn to himself, avoiding the settlements,
Sings by himself a song.

7 Song of the bleeding throat!
Death's outlet song of life—(for well, dear brother, I know,
If thou wast not gifted to sing, thou would'st surely die.)

5

8 Over the breast of the spring, the land, amid cities,
Amid lanes, and through old woods, (where lately the
     violets peep'd from the ground, spotting the gray
     debris;)
Amid the grass in the fields each side of the lanes — passing
     the endless grass;
Passing the yellow-spear'd wheat, every grain from its
     shroud in the dark-brown fields uprising;
Passing the apple-tree blows of white and pink in the
     orchards;
Carrying a corpse to where it shall rest in the grave,
Night and day journeys a coffin.

6

9 Coffin that passes through lanes and streets,
Through day and night, with the great cloud darkening the
     land,
With the pomp of the inloop'd flags, with the cities draped
     in black,

With the show of the States themselves, as of crape-veil'd
    women, standing,
With processions long and winding, and the flambeaus of
    the night,
With the countless torches lit—with the silent sea of faces,
    and the unbared heads,
With the waiting depot, the arriving coffin, and the sombre
    faces,
With dirges through the night, with the thousand voices
    rising strong and solemn;
With all the mournful voices of the dirges, pour'd around
    the coffin,
The dim-lit churches and the shuddering organs—Where
    amid these you journey,
With the tolling, tolling bells' perpetual clang;
Here! coffin that slowly passes.
I give you my sprig of lilac.

7

10 (Nor for you, for one, alone;
Blossoms and branches green to coffins all I bring:
For fresh as the morning—thus would I chant a song for
    you, O sane and sacred death.

11 All over bouquets of roses,
O death! I cover you over with roses and early lilies;
But mostly and now the lilac that blooms the first,
Copious, I break, I break the sprigs from the bushes:
With loaded arms I come, pouring for you,
For you and the coffins all of you, O death.)

8

12 O western orb, sailing the heaven!
Now I know what you must have meant, as a month since
    we walk'd,
As we walk'd up and down in the dark blue so mystic,
As we walk'd in silence the transparent shadowy night,

A*

As I saw you had something to tell, as you bent to me night
after night,
As you droop'd from the sky low down, as if to my side,
(while the other stars all look'd on ;)
As we wander'd together the solemn night, (for something
I know not what, kept me from sleep;)
As the night advanced, and I saw on the rim of the west,
ere you went, how full you were of woe ;
As I stood on the rising ground in the breeze, in the cool
transparent night,
As I watch'd where you pass'd and was lost in the nether-
ward black of the night,
As my soul, in its trouble, dissatisfied, sank, as where you,
sad orb,
Concluded, dropt in the night, and was gone.

9

13 Sing on, there in the swamp!
O singer bashful and tender! I hear your notes—I hear
your call ;
I hear—I come presently—I understand you ;
But a moment I linger—for the lustrous star has detain'd
me ;
The star, my comrade, departing, holds and detains me.

10

14 O how shall I warble myself for the dead one there I
loved ?
And how shall I deck my song for the large sweet soul that
has gone ?
And what shall my perfume be, for the grave of him I love ?

15 Sea-winds, blown from east and west,
Blown from the eastern sea, and blown from the western sea,
till there on the prairies meeting :
These, and with these, and the breath of my chant,
I perfume the grave of him I love.

11

16 O what shall I hang on the chamber walls?
And what shall the pictures be that I hang on the walls,
To adorn the burial-house of him I love?

17 Pictures of growing spring, and farms, and homes,
With the Fourth-month eve at sundown, and the gray-smoke
lucid and bright,
With floods of the yellow gold of the gorgeous, indolent,
sinking sun, burning, expanding the air;
With the fresh sweet herbage under foot, and the pale green
leaves of the trees prolific;
In the distance the flowing glaze, the breast of the river,
with a wind-dapple here and there;
With ranging hills on the banks, with many a line against
the sky, and shadows;
And the city at hand, with dwellings so dense, and stacks
of chimneys,
And all the scenes of life, and the workshops, and the
workmen homeward returning.

12

18 Lo! body and soul! this land!
Mighty Manhattan, with spires, and the sparkling and hurrying tides, and the ships;
The varied and ample land—the South and the North in
the light—Ohio's shores, and flashing Missouri,
And ever the far-spreading prairies, cover'd with grass and
corn.

19 Lo! the most excellent sun, so calm and haughty;
The violet and purple morn, with just-felt breezes:
The gentle, soft-born, measureless light;
The miracle, spreading, bathing all—the fulfill'd noon;
The coming eve, delicious—the welcome night, and the
stars,
Over my cities shining all, enveloping man and land.

13

²⁰ Sing on ! sing on, you gray-brown bird !
Sing from the swamps, the recesses—pour your chant from
      the bushes ;
Limitless out of the dusk, out of the cedars and pines.

21 Sing on, dearest brother—warble your reedy song ;
Loud human song, with voice of uttermost woe.

22 O liquid, and free, and tender !
O wild and loose to my soul ! O wondrous singer !
You only I hear ...... yet the star holds me, (but will soon
      depart ;)
Yet the lilac, with mastering odor, holds me.

14

23 Now while I sat in the day, and look'd forth,
In the close of the day, with its light, and the fields of
      spring, and the farmer preparing his crops,
In the large unconscious scenery of my land, with its lakes
      and forests,
In the heavenly aerial beauty, (after the perturb'd winds,
      and the storms ;)
Under the arching heavens of the afternoon swift passing.
      and the voices of children and women,
The many-moving sea-tides,—and I saw the ships how they
      sail'd,
And the summer approaching with richness, and the fields
      all busy with labor,
And the infinite separate houses, how they all went on, each
      with its meals and minutia of daily usages ;
And the streets, how their throbbings throbb'd, and the cities
      pent,—lo ! then and there,
Falling among them all, and upon them all, enveloping me
      with the rest,
Appear'd the cloud, appear'd the long black trail ;
And I knew Death, its thought, and the sacred knowledge
      of death.

15

24 Then with the knowledge of death as walking one side of
  me,
And the thought of death close-walking the other side of me,
And I in the middle, as with companions, and as holding the
  hands of companions,
I fled forth to the hiding receiving night, that talks not,
Down to the shores of the water, the path by the swamp in
  the dimness,
To the solemn shadowy cedars, and ghostly pines so still.

25 And the singer so shy to the rest receiv'd me;
The gray-brown bird I know, receiv'd us comrades three;
And he sang what seem'd the song of death, and a verse for
  him I love.

26 From deep secluded recesses,
From the fragrant cedars, and the ghostly pines so still,
Came the singing of the bird.

27 And the charm of the singing rapt me,
As I held, as if by their hands, my comrades in the night;
And the voice of my spirit tallied the song of the bird.

16

28 Come, lovely and soothing Death,
Undulate round the world, serenely arriving, arriving,
In the day, in the night, to all, to each,
Sooner or later, delicate Death.

29 Prais'd be the fathomless universe,
For life and joy, and for objects and knowledge curious;
And for love, sweet love—But praise! O praise and praise,
For the sure-enwinding arms of cool-enfolding Death.

30 Dark Mother, always gliding near, with soft feet,
Have none chanted for thee a chant of fullest welcome?

Then I chant it for thee—I glorify thee above all ;
I bring thee a song that when thou must indeed come, come
    unfalteringly.

31 Approach, encompassing Death—strong Deliveress !
When it is so—when thou hast taken them, I joyously sing
    the dead,
Lost in the loving, floating ocean of thee,
Laved in the flood of thy bliss, O Death.

32 From me to thee glad serenades,
Dances for thee I propose, saluting thee—adornments and
    feastings for thee ;
And the sights of the open landscape, and the high-spread
    sky, are fitting,
And life and the fields, and the huge and thoughtful night.

33 The night, in silence, under many a star ;
The ocean shore, and the husky whispering wave, whose
    voice I know ;
And the soul turning to thee, O vast and well-veil'd Death,
And the body gratefully nestling close to thee.

34 Over the tree-tops I float thee a song !
Over the rising and sinking waves—over the myriad fields,
    and the prairies wide ;
Over the dense-pack'd cities all, and the teeming wharves
    and ways,
I float this carol with joy, with joy to thee, O Death !

17

35 To the tally of my soul,
Loud and strong kept up the gray-brown bird,
With pure, deliberate notes, spreading, filling the night.

36 Loud in the pines and cedars dim,
Clear in the freshness moist, and the swamp-perfume ;
And I with my comrades there in the night.

37 While my sight that was bound in my eyes unclosed,
As to long panoramas of visions.

18

38 I saw the vision of armies;
And I saw, as in noiseless dreams, hundreds of battle-flags;
Borne through the smoke of the battles, and pierc'd with
    missiles, I saw them,
And carried hither and yon through the smoke, and torn
    and bloody;
And at last but a few shreds of the flags left on the staffs,
    (and all in silence,)
And the staffs all splinter'd and broken.

39 I saw battle-corpses, myriads of them,
And the white skeletons of young men—I saw them;
I saw the debris and debris of all dead soldiers;
But I saw they were not as was thought;
They themselves were fully at rest—they suffer'd not;
The living remain'd and suffer'd—the mother suffer'd,
And the wife and the child, and the musing comrade suf-
    fer'd,
And the armies that remain'd suffer'd.

19

40 Passing the visions, passing the night;
Passing, unloosing the hold of my comrades' hands;
Passing the song of the hermit bird, and the tallying song
    of my soul,
Victorious song, death's outlet song, (yet varying, ever-
    altering song,
As low and wailing, yet clear the notes, rising and falling,
    flooding the night,
Sadly sinking and fainting, as warning and warning, and
    yet again bursting with joy,)
Covering the earth, and filling the spread of the heaven,
As that powerful psalm in the night I heard from recesses.

20

11 Must I leave thee, lilac with heart-shaped leaves?
Must I leave thee there in the door-yard, blooming, return-
        ing with spring?

12 Must I pass from my song for thee;
From my gaze on thee in the west, fronting the west, com-
        muning with thee,
O comrade lustrous, with silver face in the night?

21

13 Yet each I keep, and all;
The song, the wondrous chant of the gray-brown bird, I keep,
And the tallying chant, the echo arous'd in my soul, I keep,
With the lustrous and drooping star, with the countenance
        full of woe;
With the lilac tall, and its blossoms of mastering odor;
Comrades mine, and I in the midst, and their memory ever
        I keep—for the dead I loved so well;
For the sweetest, wisest soul of all my days and lands…
        and this for his dear sake;
Lilac and star and bird, twined with the chant of my soul,
With the holders holding my hand, nearing the call of the
        bird,
There in the fragrant pines, and the cedars dusk and dim.

RACE OF VETERANS.

RACE of veterans!
Race of the soil, ready for conflict! race of the conquering
        march!
(No more credulity's race, abiding-temper'd race;)
Race owning no law but the law of itself;
Race of passion and the storm.

O CAPTAIN! MY CAPTAIN!

—~~—

1

O CAPTAIN! my captain! our fearful trip is done ;
The ship has weather'd every rack, the prize we sought is
    won ;
The port is near, the bells I hear, the people all exulting,
While follow eyes the steady keel, the vessel grim and daring :
      But O heart! heart! heart!
        Leave you not the little spot,
          Where on the deck my captain lies,
          Fallen cold and dead.

2

O captain! my captain! rise up and hear the bells ;
Rise·up—for you the flag is flung—for you the bugle trills ;
For you bouquets and ribbon'd wreaths—for you the shores
    a-crowding ;
For you they call, the swaying mass, their eager faces
    turning ;
      O captain! dear father!
        This arm I push beneath you ;
          It is some dream that on the deck,
          You've fallen cold and dead.

3

My captain does not answer, his lips are pale and still ;
My father does not feel my arm, he has no pulse nor will :
But the ship, the ship is anchor'd safe, its voyage closed and
    done ;
From fearful trip, the victor ship, comes in with object won :
      Exult, O shores, and ring, O bells !
        But I, with silent tread,
          Walk the spot my captain lies,
          Fallen cold and dead.

SPIRIT WHOSE WORK IS DONE.

SPIRIT whose work is done! spirit of dreadful hours!
Ere, departing, fade from my eyes your fore..ts of bayonets;
Spirit of gloomiest fears and doubts, (yet onward ever unfal-
      tering pressing;)
Spirit of many a solemn day, and many a savage scene!
      Electric spirit!
That with muttering voice, through the years now closed,
      like a tireless phantom flitted,
Rousing the land with breath of flame, while you beat and
      beat the drum;
—Now, as the sound of the drum, hollow and harsh to the
      last, reverberates round me;
As your ranks, your immortal ranks, return. return from
      the battles;
While the muskets of the young men yet lean over their
      shoulders;
While I look on the bayonets bristling over their shoulders;
While those slanted bayonets, whole forests of them, ap-
      pearing in the distance, approach and pass on, re-
      turning homeward,
Moving with steady motion, swaying to and fro, to the right
      and left,
Evenly, lightly rising and falling, as the steps keep time:
—Spirit of hours I knew, all hectic red one day, but pale as
      death next day;
Touch my mouth, ere you depart—press my lips close!
Leave me your pulses of rage! bequeath them to me! fill
      me with currents convulsive!
Let them scorch and blister out of my chants, when you are
      gone;
Let them identify you to the future in these songs.

CHANTING THE SQUARE DEIFIC.

—~~—

1

CHANTING the square deific, out of the One advancing, out
    of the sides ;
Out of the old and new—out of the square entirely divine,
Solid, four-sided, (all the sides needed) ... from this side
    JEHOVAH am I,
Old Brahm I, and I Saturnius am ;
Not Time affects me—I am Time, modern as any ;
Unpersuadable, relentless, executing righteous judgments;
As the Earth, the Father, the brown old Kronos, with laws,
Aged beyond computation—yet ever new—ever with those
    mighty laws rolling,
Relentless, I forgive no man—whoever sins, dies—: I will
    have that man's life ;
Therefore let none expect mercy—Have the seasons, gravi-
    tation, the appointed days, mercy?—No more have I ;
But as the seasons, and gravitation—and as all the appointed
    days, that forgive not,
I dispense from this side judgments inexorable, without the
    least remorse.

2

Consolator most mild, the promis'd one advancing,
With gentle hand extended, the mightier God am I,
Foretold by prophets and poets, in their most rapt proph-
    ecies and poems ;
From this side, lo! the Lord CHRIST gazes—lo! Hermes I—
    lo! mine is Hercules' face ;
All sorrow, labor, suffering, I, tallying it, absorb in myself ;
Many times have I been rejected, taunted, put in prison,
    and crucified—and many times shall be again ;
All the world have I given up for my dear brothers' and
    sisters' sake—for the soul's sake ;

Wending my way through the homes of men, rich or
    poor, with the kiss of affection ;
For I am affection—I am the cheer-bringing God, with hope,
    and all-enclosing Charity ;
(Conqueror yet—for before me all the armies and soldiers
    of the earth shall yet bow—and all the weapons of
    war become impotent :)
With indulgent words, as to children—with fresh and sane
    words, mine only ;
Young and strong I pass, knowing well I am destin'd my-
    self to an early death :
But my Charity has no death—my Wisdom dies not, neither
    early nor late,
And my sweet Love, bequeath'd here and elsewhere, never
    dies.

3

Aloof, dissatisfied, plotting revolt,
Comrade of criminals, brother of slaves,
Crafty, despised, a drudge, ignorant,
With sudra face and worn brow—black, but in the depths
    of my heart, proud as any ;
Lifted, now and always, against whoever, scorning, assumes
    to rule me ;
Morose, full of guile, full of reminiscences, brooding, with
    many wiles,
(Though it was thought I was baffled and dispell'd, and
    my wiles done—but that will never be ;)
Defiant, I, SATAN, still live—still utter words—in new lands
    duly appearing, (and old ones also ;)
Permanent here, from my side, warlike, equal with any,
    real as any,
Nor time, nor change, shall ever change me or my words.

4

Santa SPIRITA, breather, life,
Beyond the light, lighter than light,
Beyond the flames of hell—joyous, leaping easily above hell ;

Beyond Paradise—perfumed solely with mine own perfume ;
Including all life on earth—touching, including God—
    including Saviour and Satan ;
Ethereal, pervading all, (for without me, what were all ?
    what were God ?)
Essence of forms—life of the real identities, permanent,
    positive, (namely the unseen,)
Life of the great round world, the sun and stars, and of
    man—I, the general Soul,
Here the square finishing, the solid, I the most solid,
Breathe my breath also through these little songs.

⋘❦⋙

I HEARD YOU, SOLEMN-SWEET PIPES OF THE ORGAN.

I HEARD you, solemn-sweet pipes of the organ, as last
    Sunday morn I pass'd the church ;
Winds of autumn!—as I walk'd the woods at dusk, I
    heard your long-stretch'd sighs, up above, so
    mournful ;
I heard the perfect Italian tenor, singing at the opera—I
    heard the soprano in the midst of the quartet singing ;
... Heart of my love!—you too I heard, murmuring low,
    through one of the wrists around my head ;
Heard the pulse of you, when all was still, ringing little
    bells last night under my ear.

⋘❦⋙

NOT MY ENEMIES EVER INVADE ME.

NOT my enemies ever invade me—no harm to my pride from
    them I fear ;
But the lovers I recklessly love—lo! how they master me !
Lo! me, ever open and helpless, bereft of my strength !
Utterly abject, grovelling on the ground before them.

O ME! O LIFE!

O ME! O life! ... of the questions of these recurring;
Of the endless trains of the faithless—of cities fill'd with
    the foolish;
Of myself forever reproaching myself, (for who more fool-
    ish than I, and who more faithless?)
Of eyes that vainly crave the light—of the objects mean—of
    the struggle ever renew'd;
Of the poor results of all—of the plodding and sordid crowds
    I see around me;
Of the empty and useless years of the rest—with the rest me
    intertwined;
The question, O me! so sad, recurring—What good amid
    these, O me, O life?

Answer.

That you are here—that life exists, and identity;
That the powerful play goes on, and you will contribute a
    verse.

—~~~—

AH POVERTIES, WINCINGS, AND SULKY RETREATS.

Ah poverties, wincings, and sulky retreats!
Ah you foes that in conflict have overcome me!
(For what is my life, or any man's life, but a conflict with
    foes—the old, the incessant war?)
You degradations—you tussle with passions and appetites;
You smarts from dissatisfied friendships, (ah wounds, the
    sharpest of all;)
You toil of painful and choked articulations—you mean-
    nesses;
You shallow tongue-talks at tables, (my tongue the shal-
    lowest of any;)
You broken resolutions, you racking angers, you smother'd
    ennuis;
Ah, think not you finally triumph—My real self has yet to
    come forth;
It shall yet march forth o'ermastering, till all lies beneath me;
It shall yet stand up the soldier of unquestion'd victory.

AS I LAY WITH MY HEAD IN YOUR LAP, CAMERADO.

As I lay with my head in your lap, camerado,
The confession I made I resume—what I said to you and
    the open air I resume:
I know I am restless, and make others so;
I know my words are weapons, full of danger, full of death;
(Indeed I am myself the real soldier;
It is not he, there, with his bayonet, and not the red-striped
    artilleryman;)
For I confront peace, security, and all the settled laws, to
    unsettle them;
I am more resolute because all have denied me, than I could
    ever have been had all accepted me;
I heed not, and have never heeded, either experience, cau-
    tions, majorities, nor ridicule;
And the threat of what is call'd hell is little or nothing to
    me;
And the lure of what is call'd heaven is little or nothing
    to me;
... Dear camerado! I confess I have urged you onward
    with me, and still urge you, without the least idea
    what is our destination,
Or whether we shall be victorious, or utterly quell'd and
    defeated.

THIS DAY, O SOUL.

This day, O soul, I give you a wondrous mirror;
Long in the dark, in tarnish and cloud it lay—But the cloud
    has pass'd, and the tarnish gone;
... Behold, O soul! it is now a clean and bright mirror,
Faithfully showing you all the things of the world.

IN CLOUDS DESCENDING, IN MIDNIGHT SLEEP.

1

In clouds descending, in midnight sleep, of many a face of
    anguish,
Of the look at first of the mortally wounded—of that inde-
    scribable look;
Of the dead on their backs, with arms extended wide,
    I dream, I dream, I dream.

2

Of scenes of nature, the fields and the mountains;
Of the skies, so beauteous after the storm—and at night the
    moon so unearthly bright,
Shining sweetly, shining down, where we dig the trenches
    and gather the heaps,
    I dream, I dream, I dream.

3

Long have they pass'd, long lapsed—faces and trenches and
    fields;
Long through the carnage I moved with a callous compos-
    ure—or away from the fallen,
Onward I sped at the time—But now of their forms at night,
    I dream, I dream, I dream.

❧

AN ARMY ON THE MARCH.

With its cloud of skirmishers in advance,
With now the sound of a single shot, snapping like a whip,
    and now an irregular volley,
The swarming ranks press on and on, the dense brigades
    press on;
Glittering dimly, toiling under the sun, the dust-cover'd men,
In columns rise and fall to the undulations of the ground,
With artillery interspers'd—the wheels rumble, the horses
    sweat,
As the army resistless advances.

DIRGE FOR TWO VETERANS.

1

THE last sunbeam
Lightly falls from the finish'd Sabbath,
On the pavement here—and there beyond, it is looking,
　Down a new-made double grave.

2

Lo! the moon ascending!
Up from the east, the silvery round moon;
Beautiful over the house-tops, ghastly, phantom moon;
　Immense and silent moon.

3

I see a sad procession,
And I hear the sound of coming full-key'd bugles;
All the channels of the city streets they 're flooding,
　As with voices and with tears.

4

I hear the great drums pounding,
And the small drums steady whirring;
And every blow of the great convulsive drums,
　Strikes me through and through.

5

For the son is brought with the father;
(In the foremost ranks of the fierce assault they fell;
Two veterans, son and father, dropt together,
　And the double grave awaits them.)

6

Now nearer blow the bugles,
And the drums strike more convulsive;
And the day-light o'er the pavement quite has faded,
　And the strong dead-march enwraps me.

7

In the eastern sky up-buoying,
The sorrowful vast phantom moves illumin'd;
('T is some mother's large, transparent face,
     In heaven brighter growing.)

8

O strong dead-march, you please me!
O moon immense, with your silvery face you soothe me!
O my soldiers twain! O my veterans, passing to burial!
     What I have I also give you.

9

The moon gives you light,
And the bugles and the drums give you music;
And my heart, O my soldiers, my veterans,
     My heart gives you love.

HOW SOLEMN, AS ONE BY ONE.

How solemn, as one by one,
As the ranks returning, all worn and sweaty—as the men
     file by where I stand;
As the faces, the masks appear—as I glance at the faces,
     studying the masks;
(As I glance upward out of this page, studying you, dear
     friend, whoever you are;)
How solemn the thought of my whispering soul, to each in
     the ranks, and to you;
I see behind each mask, that wonder, a kindred soul:
O the bullet could never kill what you really are, dear
     friend,
Nor the bayonet stab what you really are:
... The soul! yourself I see, great as any, good as the best,
Waiting secure and content, which the bullet could never
     kill,
Nor the bayonet stab, O friend!

LO! VICTRESS ON THE PEAKS!

Lo! Victress on the peaks!
Where thou standest, with mighty brow, regarding the
          world,
(The world, O Libertad, that vainly conspired against thee;)
Out of its countless, beleaguering toils, after thwarting
          them all;
Where thou, dominant, with the dazzling sun around thee,
Towerest now unharm'd, in immortal soundness and bloom—
          lo! in this hour supreme,
No poem proud I, chanting, bring to thee—nor mastery's
          rapturous verse;
But a little book, containing night's darkness, and blood-
          dripping wounds,
And psalms of the dead.

RECONCILIATION.

WORD over all, beautiful as the sky!
Beautiful that war, and all its deeds of carnage, must in
          time be utterly lost;
That the hands of the sisters Death and Night, incessantly
          softly wash again, and ever again, this soil'd world:
... For my enemy is dead—a man divine as myself is dead;
I look where he lies, white-faced and still, in the coffin—I
          draw near;
I bend down and touch lightly with my lips the white face
          in the coffin.

TO THE LEAVEN'D SOIL THEY TROD.

To the leaven'd soil they trod, calling, I sing, for the last :
(Not cities, nor man alone, nor war, nor the dead,
But forth from my tent emerging for good—loosing, unty-
    ing the tent-ropes;)
In the freshness, the forenoon air, in the far-stretching cir-
    cuits and vistas, again to peace restored,
To the fiery fields emanative, and the endless vistas beyond—
    to the south and the north ;
To the leaven'd soil of the general western world, to attest
    my songs,
(To the average earth, the wordless earth, witness of war
    and peace,)
To the Alleghanian hills, and the tireless Mississippi,
To the rocks I, calling, sing, and all the trees in the woods,
To the plain of the poems of heroes, to the prairie spreading
    wide,
To the far-off sea, and the unseen winds, and the sane im-
    palpable air ;
... And responding, they answer all, (but not in words.)
The average earth, the witness of war and peace, acknowl-
    edges mutely ;
The prairie draws me close, as the father, to bosom broad,
    the son ;
The Northern ice and rain, that began me, nourish me
    to the end ;
But the hot sun of the South is to ripen my songs.

FINIS.